A Gift to Others

Will Your Life be a Gift to Others?

Stephen Ong M.D.

A GIFT TO OTHERS

Will Your Life be a Gift to Others?

STEPHEN ONG, M.D.

Kravitz & Sons

INNOVATORS IN PUBLISHING, MARKETING AND ADVERTISING

Kravitz and Sons LLC
204 E Arlington Blvd. Suite B
Greenville, NC 27858

Published by Kravitz and Sons LLC.

ISBN: 979-8-89639-641-3 (sc)
ISBN: 979-8-89639-640-6 (e)

Table Of Contents

FOREWORD i

INTRODUCTION iii

CHAPTER ONE: The Gift 1

CHAPTER TWO: Relationships 7

CHAPTER THREE: Family 18

CHAPTER FOUR: Vision 26

CHAPTER FIVE: Wisdom 37

CHAPTER SIX: Effort 44

CHAPTER SEVEN: Stewardship..................................50

CHAPTER EIGHT: Success..56

CHAPTER NINE: Work..64

CHAPTER TEN: Blessing...77

CONCLUSION...81

FOREWORD

Years ago, I had a church secretary who liked to say, "Don't forget, Pastor Ray, have a blast while you last." And if she forgot to say it to me, I would say it to her. I always thought that little saying summed up an enormous spiritual truth. Since we won't be here forever, we might as well have a blast while we last. Folk singer Joan Baez put it this way: "You don't get to choose how you're going to die or when. You only get to choose how you're going to live now."

Underneath the name of any gravestone in any cemetery, you will see something like this:

1936-2004

A date of birth, a date of death, and a dash to represent everything in between.

That's all this life really is—the short little "–" between the time we show up and the time we depart. Either that thought makes us depressed or inspires us to action, perhaps we should put the question this way: What are you doing with the dash? How will you fill the "–" that will reflect your life on earth?

In this fine book, my friend Stephen Ong asks us to consider carefully how we will answer that question. As you read his story, you'll discover what it means to view your life as a gift from God meant to be shared with others.

God never gives his blessings to be hoarded. He gives them to us so that we will give them to others. This is the very essence of Christianity.

From God To us To others

Have you ever gone to a pond out in the country and thrown a pebble into the water? What happens? From the point where the pebble enters the water, ripples spread out farther and farther. What starts as a ripple from one small pebble soon affects the whole pond.

Stephen Ong's amazing story illustrates the "pebble principle" beautifully. He looks for opportunities to bless others, and the ripples spread out in all directions. Let me make one bold prediction right now. If you read this book with an open heart, it might just change the way you live your life. Stephen not only shows us how to live; he gives us both the inspiration and the practical help we need.

Prepare to be blessed and challenged. Then go out and make your life a gift to others.

Dr. Ray Pritchard
President, Keep Believing Ministries

Author: *An Anchor for the Soul, Stealth Attack, and He's God and We're Not.*

INTRODUCTION

Throughout my life, I wondered, as many do, just what I was doing here in this world . . . what value did I have in the scheme of things. Later, when I was older studying medicine, and later still when I grew into a man, living and working as a physician, I could never get away from that primary question: What was I doing here? What was my life worth? I know that I came into this world with nothing, yet when I look around me, I now see all of the beautiful things in my life. I see a lovely wife, family, friends, memories, a successful medical career, and a thriving medical research center. I see all of these things as gifts from others, as gifts from God. In truth, my friends, family, and mentors have gifted me with love, affection, friendship, and even financial opportunities throughout my life. And yet is this the true measure of what my life is worth? Join me as I tell you a story of a lifetime of receiving and giving gifts, what value gifts from others have brought to my life, and how I ultimately reconciled myself to my role of being "a gift to others."

I have written this book because I believe that I have been blessed with the gift of life and have attempted to live obediently according to the gifts and talents our Creator has given me. At this point in my life, I have achieved a measure of "success" with my family, with my work, and within my community at large. I want to share what I have learned during my time on earth through both my failures and my successes.

I am not the wealthiest, most successful, or happiest man on earth, but my life "works." What I have found is that the most important thing we do in life is to consider ourselves, our very lives, to be a gift to others.

Every man, woman, and child on earth today has something to give; each one of us is a gift to be given the people in our lives. The problem is we do not see ourselves this way.

This book is a humble effort to show you how to visualize yourself as a gift to others in every situation in life. It is about training yourself to see how you can help, inspire, and encourage others by becoming a gift to them. In so doing, you will find the key to happiness. The book is about real-life stories, which are used as a springboard to show the importance of having a positive relationship that makes you a gift to others.

Some of the names mentioned in the book are real, while others are fictitious to protect the individual's identity

It is about living a life based on Christian principle. It is about a balanced life. It is about being obedient to our Lord; however, it is not about salvation.

On the negative side, we see that the world today has a dire prognosis with faltering economies, compromised teaching institutions, weakened military, corrupt leaders, abused children, the discarded elderly, the disregarded sick, failing governments, celebrity's/celebrities' achievement not celebrated?, and the word "hope" seems like a bad joke. Western civilization itself is under threat.

So it would almost seem to be saccharine for our book to ask the question: "Is your life a gift to other people?"

And yet we know there's something inherently true about this question. We know it because we know the selfish narcissism of our culture has produced a fruit that has eaten away at the fabric of people's lives.

The question remains:

Would you dare to be a gift to others in your life?

Would you dare to put your needs and concerns behind the needs and concerns of other people?

Would you dare to give your life away no matter what your given vocations or talents are?

And even with all this, most likely your answer would be "No! There is no payoff!"

If you answered this way, this book is dedicated to you.

This is my humble attempt to share my understanding of how to live a life that matters. It is a blessing that should be passed on from generation to generation.

> When I was a four-year-old growing up in Indonesia, I was just beginning to awaken to the world around me. My world was slowly growing brighter from the dim, vague awareness of my parents' house; my mother and father's love; and the safe, everyday routine of playing, eating, and sleeping. Soon my first perceptions were replaced with a burning curiosity of what lay behind the front door. At first, everything seemed to begin with the word "No!" As my father always seemed to be away on business, my mother soon began taking me and other children for walks through the neighborhood. Sometimes, when she opened the door for us in the morning, the cool dark interior of our house would be replaced by morning sunlight so bright that the whole world disappeared into a dazzling white glare. We would walk, and she would point out the people and places of our neighborhood.
>
> "There is the church, here is a friendly next-door neighbor, and this is how you safely cross the street." Around one particular corner, a man sold ice cream out of a brightly colored pushcart every day. The cart had three shiny containers on top from which he scooped out different flavors. My mother and I would stop, and she would treat me to a scoop of homemade ice cream in a small sugar cone. The flavors were unique to this vendor. Some were bright purple in color, others luscious tan, and yet others were a startling orange and green. All were delicious to me. They tasted so fresh and sweet—like nothing else in my world—of

native Indonesian fruit, special desserts, and exotic flavors. When I close my eyes and think back, I can taste them still, like it was only yesterday. I thought ice cream to be the most wonderful gift in the world and hoped that life would be just one ice cream gift to me after another. I was soon to learn otherwise.

CHAPTER ONE

The Gift

L et's begin with the basic question: What is a gift? For many
months now, I've been puzzling over an adequate answer to
this question. In my own lifetime, I have given and received many
gifts. There are, after all, many definitions for the word "gift." The
dictionary offers three suggestions:

1. Something that is bestowed voluntarily and without
   compensation
2. The act, right, or power of giving
3. A talent, endowment, aptitude, or inclination

The common perception, the definition that children so commonly
hold dear, is the first one: something that is bestowed voluntarily
and without compensation. We buy into this idea every holiday and
birthday, especially for children. We give gifts or presents to meet
someone's needs or celebrate some event. For this book, however, I
want to focus on how we, ourselves, can become gifts to one another
in ways other than merely bestowing trinkets.

A gift must be valuable to both the giver and the receiver, or it
is not a gift. Everyone, rich or poor, smart or dumb, knows how to
evaluate what a gift is truly worth. A gift's value is relative to one
thing—the one who is giving it. To give away five dollars may mean
the difference between life and death to a poor man. He may not be
able to eat that day if he gives away his last five dollars. To a rich
man, five dollars is not a valuable sum. To a busy man, giving an
hour of his day is very significant.

But we still have two more definitions to consider. There is the act,
right, and power of giving, and then there is also the talent.

1

Why should we give? Well, let's consider that question from the opposite angle. Why should we not give? Why not just play Scrooge and hoard not only our wealth, but also our friendship and time? Dickens taught us that because he withheld himself from his community, Scrooge was a wealthy but very unhappy man. His life was devoted to moneymaking alone. I doubt there are many people who want to spend their lives that way. I think you get what you give.

Our parents are gifts to us—they take care of us and lead the way to healthy, mature living. By the same token, we can be gifts to our children by taking the time to be there for their activities and hobbies.

For example, I have always endeavored to attend my son's baseball games. One year, I received a phone call a few weeks after tryouts for his Little League team. One of the volunteers for the league was on the other end of the line.

"Stephen," he said, "there are so many children involved in the league this year that we need to make an additional team." My son was one of the children chosen by lottery to be on this new team.

"I've seen you around every year. I know you try to make it to all your son's games. This new team needs a coach. We were thinking you could help out, if you are available. So what do you say?" he asked me.

"I would love to do it, but I don't think I can coach. I don't know all the rules of the game." At the time, I knew very little about the sport. I went to all the games, but the rules were a mystery to me. All I knew was that there were three strikes and that the boys used bats to hit the ball. That was seriously just about the extent of my knowledge. "If someone else will coach, I can help out with the team," I told him. So in the end, they made me the manager of the team. I did not want to have a detrimental effect on the team's success, but I still wanted to be there for my son.

We practiced every week, and we played as scheduled. We had some fun times together, and we had some not-so-good times as well, but we encouraged each other, and we screamed and we clapped. For my son and me, it was both good quality time and bonding time together. The team ended up in the championship that year. Looking back, I know that my son was grateful for the time that I spent with him and his team.

That is the kind of giving I want to address in this book. You can be a gift in every aspect of your life, and in turn, others can be gifts to you in ways you might not foresee. You might find gifts in the most unusual places. One night, your car might hit a nail and get a flat tire. That person who stops to help you change the flat tire is a gift. And if that person inspires you to go out and help someone else, then they have made you into a gift, too. A gift can be as mundane and obvious as simply treating your employees well and giving them a fair salary.

Helen Keller once wrote, "The most pathetic person in the world is someone who has sight, but has no vision." Talents are gifts from God and must not be taken lightly. They should be developed and used appropriately. While not always the case, I think a talent often steers the individual toward the career that will make them most happy. If your passion is teaching, then do not be dissuaded from that career path toward another that pays more money or seems easier.

Being a gift to others starts by being a gift to yourself. In order to be a gift, you must first know who you are. Our talents determine who we are at the core of our identity. In order to become a gift, you must know who you are.

"As a man thinketh in his heart, so he is" —Proverbs 23:7

Without ever having met you, I already know who you are. You are exactly the person whom you believe yourself to be. How you see yourself, how you think about yourself, the image you hold in your mind of yourself—this is who you are. And becoming a gift to others starts with seeing yourself as that gift.

So let's begin with how we see ourselves; let's begin with personal identity.

Primarily, we see ourselves through our relationship; our identity is revealed through relationships. What this means is other people reflect back to us, through interaction, a sense of who we are in the world. Children learn very quickly who they are by whom their parents reflect them to be. We identify who we are in this way, through relationship, and first and foremost through family relationships.

The family is the place where we are first imprinted with a sense of identity—a sense of self—through our relationships with our parents, siblings, and extended family. We also learn to interact in life in line with the ways we first related to our parents, siblings, and other immediate family members. The way we relate is through our role in the family.

So we are initially defined by our place in the family, as the family is the foundation of all other relationships we build in life. How we learn who we are in our family unit is by learning to play our role—how to be an older brother, youngest son, middle daughter, or only child in relationship to our parents, other siblings, and other immediate family members. These roles we learn in our family relationships are the foundation we build on as we relate to others in the workplace, our school, our community, and our recreational and religious lives as well.

No matter where you are today regarding your immediate family members, how you see yourself primarily will be related to your family role. Even if you are single, you still define yourself, identify yourself, or see yourself in some manner by your family relationships, widower, single mom, or single dad. This primary family identity or role is one of the most important parts of how you see yourself and will be part of how to expand the way you think about yourself as a gift.

In this brief span of our life, the best way to move forward is to get along with your companions on the journey. Be a gift to yourself, be a gift to others. This book is about vision, wisdom, success, relationships, balance, family, stewardship, work, and the ultimate blessing.

The first gift a person can receive is the gift of life itself, followed by the gift of long or short life on earth. Life is an opportunity to be a gift to oneself and a gift to others. During our lives, we also have an opportunity to receive the gift of salvation—the ultimate gift.

In the pages of this book, I will endeavor to explore what it means to be a gift to others and the variety of outcomes that can be expected in different circumstances. How do we reach a win-win outcome? What does it mean to be a gift to yourself? The answers to these questions affect every aspect of life.

When I was old enough to go to school, during my early high school year, I was becoming a rather spoiled young man. My outlook was all one-sided. I just wanted everything given to me without any effort wasted on any return. Then my parents decided to send me to a particular American school which turned to be a Seventh-Day Adventist school. Located on the other side of the island, they taught students to appreciate the benefits of hard work. At first, this was a living nightmare for me. Having come from a sheltered, if not pampered environment, I was now expected to do my share of cleaning, digging in the gardens, and other manual forms of yard work. It was simply intolerable. I absolutely refused until I felt the scorn of all the other students who did their fair share of work. So I began to pitch in, doing small jobs and less difficult work. Soon, bit by bit, my body began to adjust to the physical effort. In days, I discovered that vigorous workouts made my body feel good.

My young, physical form responded favorably and filled out with lean muscles and increased stamina. My attitude changed. I lost the spoiled brat mentality. I became a model worker with an appreciation and zest for arduous work. I began to understand that, without giving my heartfelt efforts, I would never have received these wonderful new benefits of health, stamina, and perspective on life. With my first pay, I bought my grandmother some fine-blue dress cloth. She shed tears when I gave it to her. She was so happy that I was growing up from a young child who only wanted to take, to a maturing grandson who had made her a gift from his first paycheck. For the first time, I began to understand that, when building relationships, it is best to give rather than just to receive. And that in all things, what you may get is equal to what you will give.

CHAPTER TWO
Relationships

Many years ago, my wife was saddened by the resignation of our former pastor of the church we attended. For all those years, his teaching and preaching had blessed us. We had had good relationship, getting together for times of fellowship and having meals together, and we had been sharing words of encouragement with each other. We had such a great relationship to the extent that he married us. We were both sad when he left because we did not foresee his departure. On the surface, everything looked fine and well, and had no inkling that something might be wrong. However, the reason he resigned was not the source of our sadness. What saddened us was the fact that we did not express our appreciation as much as we should.

We did not show enough encouragement to him. We did not write thank-you notes of encouragement. Once he announced his resignation, we felt it was a little too late to do those right things. My wife feels that we need to do more for our pastors and our church leaders to let them know how much we appreciate them.

"What we need to do is to express frequently the gift of encouragement to each other."

Every conversation and encounter constitutes a relationship of some sort. The nature of these relationships varies widely, but that does not change the fact that you should be, at the very least, cordial in each and every interaction with others.

How would you want to be treated? Say you are on the phone. You are trying to order a cake for your daughter's birthday party. The baker on the line explains the different designs, but says they don't have any more chocolate cakes right now—and you need the cake today. Should you get angry and passive-aggressive, the baker may treat your daughter's cake with far less care. It is not this person's fault that they are out of chocolate cakes. If you react in anger, you have just fostered a lose-lose relationship.

It is important to be polite to people in the service industry, but more important to each of us are the relationships that hold great meaning in our lives. We all have people in our lives, who are very dear to us, and who give value to our lives. These people shape us and bring us joy into our lives.

There are people in our lives that we know are there only because of the gift of Providence, and by virtue of this, they are "spiritual family." It is one of life's most humbling moments to know you are receiving a gift of a relationship that rises to the level of your family. These people usually are gifts of transformation to us because, as they have been gifts to us, they inspire us to be a gift ourselves.

One of the most important gifts I've had in my life was a relationship with someone to whom I was not related, but who gave me gifts that only a family member would give. Our relationship helped shape me into who I am today.

There is one man in my life in particular who deserves mention. I am talking about Mr. Carrigan. He died several years ago, but he was a true friend and business partner.

He is the man who sold me the plot of land on which I established my medical center.

At first, I wasn't sure I was ever actually going to meet Mr. Carrigan. You see, I had a vision for my medical career years ago; I wanted to build and establish a medical center. Moreover, Mr. Carrigan owned the plot of land that I wished to purchase. My brother Rio resourcefully helped my real estate agent track down Mr. Carrigan, only for us to find he did not want to sell the land. The plot was vacant and next to another parcel that had a restaurant on it. It was perfectly situated for my needs and for traffic flow for a medical center.

But all calls to Mr. Carrigan went unanswered, and the word around town was he did not want, or need, to sell. My real estate agent was very persistent, however. He called all around town to try to contact Mr. Carrigan to no avail. He called at his home repeatedly, with no answer, until one day, Mr. Carrigan happened to answer himself when my agent called. (This was in the days before everyone had answering machines and available 24/7 on their cell phones!) That call was the beginning of our relationship.

I will never forget the first time I met him. A meeting was arranged at his home, and I was a little surprised at what I found there. Mr. Carrigan was a very rich man, but you wouldn't know it by the way he lived. He dressed casually and lived a comfortable, but very simple life. He did not drive an expensive car, and while his home was spacious, you could see he didn't care much for extravagance.

When I arrived, he introduced himself and led me to his study, which was a warm, but quiet room with lots of pictures on the walls. Once we sat down, he asked me to tell him about the medical center I was thinking of building. He wanted to know what kind of medicine I practiced and what kinds of people I was looking to help.

"Well, I am family practice doctor. I want to open a medical center rather than a small, private practice. I would like to eventually have several doctors in my building, so we can serve as many people as possible," I explained.

Mr. Carrigan then told me a little bit about himself. There were three things that were near and dear to his heart: China, religion, and the practice of medicine. He had done charitable work in China, he was a very strong Catholic, and he was enthusiastic about the medical field as a benefit to mankind.

So we were a match made in heaven, as they say, because: I am Chinese, I am a believing Christian, and I love the medical field as a physician myself.

"It was all Providential timing."

I was completely surprised, however, when Mr. Carrigan proceeded to tell me that he would give the land to me if I gave the money to a charitable organization of his choosing. "Don't go to the bank," he implored.

Instead, Mr. Carrigan wanted to finance the whole thing, privately, acting as the bank himself. He wanted me to donate the money to Catholic University, and he sold me the land with a discount. He even offered to finance the construction of the building with his private mortgage. With the assistance of my real estate agent, we organized all of the paperwork, and we had a deal.

What a blessing to me for having that kind of relationship. This allowed me to start a long-range plan for the land; we set up a small building that we could expand in stages, thus, keeping total costs down over time to complete my vision for a medical center.

What I thought was a real estate transaction turned out to be Mr. Carrigan's way of teaching me about charity. He not only gave to charities and nonprofit organizations, but he taught us younger people the importance of giving back to our community. He convinced me to donate the money, and in doing so, he taught me how making such donations are important not just for the community, but also for the soul. You feel it deep down when you've done something good for your community. It is a sense of goodness that never leaves your heart.

Over time, Mr. Carrigan became a good friend and in some ways a role model to me. He was a gift to me, and I don't mean just financially as you can see. I like to think that I was gift to him in return in some measure as well. I never missed a mortgage payment, although he would call me up and ask, "Stephen? How are you doing this month?"

If I said the month had not been going particularly well, he would tell me, "Well, don't worry about the payment this month. Just get it to me when you have it."

I tried never to take advantage of this, but it was very generous of him to work with me in this way.

Mr. Carrigan is the type of man I aspire to be because he became a gift to me. He was an example to me in many important ways. He became for me a standard of how to be a benefactor in our community, how to use your finances to help people, and how to not squander your money by living high. He used his time on earth to be an angel to those who needed help. He was a gift to everyone. I saw him interact within his life, and he was a most powerful and crucial gift to me personally.

Mr. Carrigan is the kind of man I want to become. He maintained good relationships with everyone he knew. He was a great philanthropist to the community, always donating money or helping people. He did not hoard like a greedy Scrooge. He used his time on earth to be an angel to those who needed it. He was a gift to everyone. Both Mr. Carrigan and my wife are of Irish descent. Our families had a lot in common, and we became close. He was a gift to our family.

Mr. Carrigan got sick as he got older. The priests he knew would often stop by his house to take care of him. To me, this was an example of the blessed relationship of his philanthropy. He had spent much of his life "taking care" of the church through large contributions to Catholic institutions, so when he became sick, the church took care of him. He exemplifies the idea of "being a gift" and instilled in me, through his example, this life changing idea.

Unintentionally, I found myself in a close relationship with Mr. Carrigan because his acts of kindness to me regarding the fulfillment of my dream to build a medical center were only possible because of his gifting the land to me. What he did was something that usually only family members do for one another.

Perhaps he needed a "son" like me in some way, as he and his wife were childless. This was borne out in an interesting manner. He wanted me to purchase his large home in Little Washington, a home where, every Fourth of July, he would throw a huge celebration for the entire community.

It was the highlight of the year for the town. Hundreds of people from around the area came to his home to watch the parade, listen to the music, and take in the fireworks show. By offering me his home to purchase, I knew he would be giving me another wonderful financial deal if I chose to buy. But I also knew what he was offering me was more than just a piece of real estate this time. He wanted me, in some fashion, to follow in his footsteps, as I understood what he wanted to bequeath to me. He knew I understood his life better than most, and it was his desire as a "father" to me that I "inherited" his home or took over his position in the community.

My life was very full with growing children and a growing medical center at that point in time, and it would not have worked to uproot us all to move to his home. As lovely as it was, and as wonderful as I'm sure his terms would have been, it would not have worked out for me and my family for both logistical and practical reasons.

As you might imagine, the gift of Mr. Carrigan was most probably the foremost gift in my life, outside that of my family. His gift enlightens my worldview to this day. By making charitable and community contributions part of our original business deal, a part of the deal I thought was perhaps slightly eccentric at the time, he instilled in me the understanding of what it means to be a leading member of the community—a gift to me that has paid off in infinite ways since.

Mr. Carrigan became a model to me in one of the most important ways by his "gift" to me, though I did not realize it entirely at the time. He led by example, and he taught me by his generosity; the gift of Mr. Carrigan affected me in a way that I wanted to be as much like him as possible.

Because he was not, in strict terms, my family, his gift to me actually became dearer, more precious. In a way, Mr. Carrigan's gift was probably my unconscious impetus for this book.

Another important relationship we have is not with other people, but with our country. The United States is still the land of opportunity. Every year, more immigrants want to come to the US because they see America as the Promised Land. In this country, everyone is born with a clean slate, tabula rasa. We all receive a free education and a chance to succeed. No matter what your background is, if you are an American, you have that chance because everyone is equal in the eyes of the law. I am an immigrant, and I am proud to be a US citizen.

I do not know if I could have done so well in any other country. Look at Sonia Sotomayor. After President Obama appointed her as a justice on the Supreme Court, the press interviewed her. She said that she is a daughter of immigrants. The United States provided her with a great education, which opened up many possibilities for her. This is why her parents came to this country. They wanted to give their children every chance at success. America is indeed a promised land that evens up the playing field to allow anyone the opportunity to become a judge, a president, and a doctor. I agree with her perspective.

The United States is a gift to me, and I think I am a gift to my adopted country through my medical center and general good citizenry. It is a win-win situation and part of what makes our country great. I strive to help people and be a good neighbor.

We all want to succeed, and in this country, we can. But there are those who abuse our country. They take advantage of the welfare system, becoming a strain on the taxpayers around them so that they can stay home and be lazy. This is the alternative, and it is not a win-win. This does not take into account those individuals who are in real need and truly need a helping hand.

I believe in working hard and in equal opportunity for every citizen of the country. We should not depend on "bail out," but we should each do our best and use the gift of labor. Ecclesiastes says we do well if we enjoy our work, which is a gift of God.

You cannot be a gift to your country if you abuse the system for your own slothful gain. It is a sad fact of life because it is hard to weed out those who do not actually need the welfare from those who do. One time, my wife tried to help a homeless person on the street.

A man and his wife or girlfriend standing on the side of the road with a sign requesting money for food. My wife had food in her car, so she gave it to them.

"We asked for money!" the man shouted and threw the food away. There were clearly ulterior motives at work here. My wife was trying to do a good deed, but she was attempting to help someone who did not want her particular brand of "help."

It makes me sad to see people like these who let their potential flow down the drain in favor of taking advantage of others and their country. It is unhealthy and not based on the natural give-and-take that so many of us have, not only with our country, but also friends and family. This is a relationship based on take-take-take.

An old proverb says, "If you give a man a fish, he will eat for a day. But if you teach a man to fish, he can eat every day." You can see the two types of relationships at play in this old adage. One is based on win-lose and the other on win-win.

This is why education is so important. We put away enough money for the children's education. We met their needs, and we tried not to spoil them. We can help people by teaching them to help themselves. This is a principle that my wife and I live by as we have educated our children. We do not want them to rely on us forever, but rather to rely on themselves and learn how to become responsible adults. Now that they are adults, they thank us for this brand of tutelage.

Family is the foundation for human relationships. We learn how to interact with others as we build relationships with our siblings and parents. As a father, I was careful to develop a solid foundation of support for my children. The end result was win-win.

My wife and I experience great joy from our children, and we are gifts to them. Unfortunately, the reality is that some do not have that kind of positive relationship with their children.

There is a family that is very dear to me. I knew them well. The father had a successful career and had a significant position in his company. However, he had not established a win-win relationship with his family. The relationship between the father and the children was not positive, with one exception. The father was attached to one of his sons. The father showed favoritism among the children, and that caused an uneasy relationship for the entire family.

The father did not spend quality, much less quantity, and time with his children. Before the mother died, the parents had a will that divided the property and other assets equally among the six children.

Following the death of the mother, the father expressed a few times verbally and also in writing by scratching on a piece of paper informally—to the discontent of his children—that the property should be given to his favorite son. However, before the father died, no one believed that the actual will had been changed. Once the father died, a new will surfaced, showing that all of the property would indeed go only to his favorite son. The final will had not previously been revealed to the other children.

This is the kind of situation that often leads to family feuds. This sort of relationship is lose-lose. The father's expressed favoritism alienated his other children, and with this newly written will, he left his family in an awkward situation.

Fortunately, the favorite son, out of his kindness of heart, devised a plan to divide the property equally among the siblings. His generosity was a gift to his siblings.

While that story did have a happy ending, it also had the potential for total devastation of the family. Parents must be equitable in the treatment of their children. It is not fair to express favoritism and neglect some members of the family. Relationships within the family are the most important relationships you can have. These are the people who are bound to love you unconditionally and support you no matter what you do.

We have other relationships as well at our workplaces, churches, and businesses we patronize. How would we support and pray for missionaries without an ongoing relationship?

The relationship between the physicians and the pharmaceutical representatives used to focus on the mutual respect and understanding. But recently, we noticed the relationship was based primarily on sale and promotion of the products. That approach has been counterproductive.

James Dean was a person I tried to imitate during my early high school days. I became another rebel without a cause, or maybe I was just a rebel without a clue. I wore my hair flat and slicked back—just like James's. Tight Levi jeans were what all the boys were sporting along with leather jackets. I even badgered my parents about getting me a motorcycle. But no dice—all I got was a nice Vespa scooter, very good for transportation, but not so good for being Mr. Cool. When I was nearly expelled for partying rather than studying, my parents had enough. They pulled me out of school and put me in the "American school" on the other side of the island. This turned out to be a gift in disguise, for this school was actually a Seventh-Day Adventist mission school run by American teachers and principal. This man helped change my attitude, and as a result, changed my life. The Seventh-Day Adventist ran some of the finest hospitals in Southeast Asia. With this American's guidance, my hero-as-clueless rebel was replaced by a higher ideal. All of my younger years, I had naturally assumed that I would automatically be a businessman like my older brothers. So it greatly surprised me when my mother took me aside to have a serious talk. She told me that I was different from my brothers; not in a bad way. It was just that my perspective was different. My natural temperament was one that tended to help and care for everyone I happened to meet. My mother said I would not make a good businessman because of this. Conversely, she proclaimed that I would naturally make an excellent doctor because caring was at the core of being a doctor. I did not understand this at first, as I wanted to be like my brothers. But I eventually accepted the fact that I was indeed the kind of person that looked after the health and well-being of others. Like the teacher who ran my school, she gave me an insight into my character, and it was a gift that changed my life and put me on the path to success as a medical professional in the United States.

CHAPTER THREE

Family

It is well and good to be successful in your career, education, and life, but family is what makes everything else worthwhile. My family is the most important part of my life. I am one of many children. I am a husband, a father to four children, and a grandfather of three grandchildren. My family is the inspiration for everything I do.

The Bible says, "God places people in families"—that he chooses our families for us. If we really believe this, then our eyes will be opened to seeing those in our family with special eyes, a new awareness that each family member is a uniquely wrapped present for us.

God chose each one of your relatives to be a gift for you, and you to be a gift for them! Each one of your family members is a gift in some way; each reflects back to you something unique—at the same time defined by boundaries of your relationship role.

No one chooses their family, and all of us find ourselves cast in a role of some sort within them. Sometimes this makes us look at our family as commonplace or something that we take for granted. But you must see your family and your role within it as a gift because that's what it is.

With a new awareness of how you primarily see yourself today in terms of a family role, think about how this affects or changes relationships you have with members of your family today. If you recently had a baby, your primary role might be that of mother, and it will affect your husband as his wife and other members of your family.

But when I was young and foolish, I could not say the same. I loved my family, of course, but teenagers are often selfish creatures. I was rebellious, as many teenagers are. We often rebel at that age because we want to be like our friends and desire to do anything than schoolwork. We do not see that our parents are looking out for our best interests.

At fifteen, I was too busy partying and having fun to take a serious interest in my coursework. To set me straight, my parents sent me to a reform school on the other side of Indonesia. I don't think I knew it at the time, but it was a Seventh-Day Adventist school designed to help children get back on track. I didn't even know that it was a reform school. I was just excited to get to "travel" a bit; see the other side of the country. I selfishly saw this as the opportunity for more freedom from my parents and their rules. In the end, this was a gift to both my parents and me.

One summer, the school remained open to allow students to work. The money wasn't good, but teenagers don't need a lot of money to get around. So I stayed on and worked all summer. I was essentially digging ditches because the school was planning to expand its campus, but I learned the virtue of working hard. I would have to say that this school turned my life around, as I am sure it did the lives of many others.

This was the first time that I had worked for money. I still remember what the teacher told me as she handed over the paycheck. "Stephen, use this money for a good cause." I didn't ask her why. Instead, I listened. I could see it in her eyes; she wanted to teach me the importance of not being wasteful with one's money.

The other lesson was obviously that I should be a force of good in this world; I should use the money to help someone or perhaps save it. I thought of another teacher in my life, my grandmother. My grandmother was an important part of my early childhood. She lived with my family, and she often told me stories. She would read the Bible daily with me by her side, helping establish a very strong foundation early in my life.

The stories she shared were actually parables and lessons from the Bible, so I became acquainted with religious ideals at an early age. My grandmother was a religious and thrifty old woman who made her clothes by hand. So I picked out this beautiful blue fabric and purchased it for her with that first paycheck since I knew blue was her favorite color. My gift made her very happy.

That cloth was the first real gift I'd ever given, and it felt good to do something nice for her. With my first earnings, I learned both the value of money and the value of giving. I remember my grandmother exclaiming, "My son never did anything like this for me, but my grandson did!" The school enabled me to be both a gift to my grandmother as well as a gift to myself. It made me feel good to do something for her. Working hard at that school got me back on track with my studies, helping me to move forward with my plan to become a doctor, just as my mother knew I should.

When I was a young boy, she told me, "Stephen, you should be a doctor. Business does not suit you. You are too kind for it." She did not mean to say that my brothers were unkind but simply that my talents seemed to point me away from business as a career. I was not slick enough to be a smart businessman. My brothers, on the other hand, are very good at that sort of thing. They are clever enough for the family business.

My mother was a great guide to me, and I know that I made her happy by becoming a successful physician. My siblings and I were blessed with a mother who had vision and wisdom. She was a gift to us.

When family relationships are strong, parents strive to make the best life possible for their children, and when they succeed, all are happy. It makes me extremely happy to see my own children pursuing their talents. That is why I strive to be there for them in every way.

Whenever one of our children started at a new school, my wife and I drive them to the new school and help them get settled in. We even did this for my daughter when she moved to the Caribbean Islands to study. We flew down with her and spent a few days making sure that she would be happy in her new environment.

I know that my children appreciate the support we give them because I appreciated my own family's support in my endeavors. My mother once told my brothers and sisters and me this: "I want to make sure when you all grow up that you help any sibling that might be in need, whether they are older or younger than you." It was very important to her that we, as a family unit, would support each other and take care of each other whenever one of us might be in need. I ask the same of my own children.

My entire family has been successful, and I truly believe it is because of our mother's lessons. My older sister Sylvia helped support me when I was in medical school. She sacrificed her own dreams during those years by helping me rather than going to medical school herself, which she really wanted to do. After completing my medical degree and beginning my internship in Maryland, I was able to live with her for a while. That was a real gift. She is a gift to me.

While my brother was in medical school, I bought him a house. That is how we live. That is how we get by. We take care of one another. During my earlier years, I did not have much interaction with my oldest sister and my youngest sister. That was only because they both lived far away from me. As we were growing up, we became closer.

My younger sister Joan was a caring person, and she always made sure each of us was taken care of. My other younger brother and I were in restaurant business together while he was running the family business. He made sure that I got my share of the profits each month. By offering each other material and emotional support, we have helped each other get through everything. What could be more important?

I may not have had the opportunity get to know my oldest and my youngest sisters, but my recent trip to visit Indonesia have provided me the insight on how sweet and how caring they are to each of the siblings. I was given the gift of growing closer to them and appreciating even more the blessing of family.

Does that familial bond have to remain strictly within the ties of blood? I would say no, not at all. Families find themselves in many different situations.

Of course, there are negative situations and abusive families. Constant fighting between the parents cannot be good for a child. Children in abusive homes often grow up to be abusive themselves or criminally dangerous. So we see that these kinds of home situations are in no way win-win. They are in fact lose-lose.

Sometimes foster families provide more positive home environments and the relationships a child experiences with them are more akin to real familial ties. There are children who grow up with the gift of wonderful foster parents. These people are more like parents than the birth parents. The best gift you can give to a child is a supportive and loving home where he feels safe and happy.

Several years ago, my wife and I took in a friend's daughter for a few months while she interned at a local company. Aimee was a brilliant girl, very warm and intelligent. She wanted to pay rent to us because she kept a room in our home and took family meals with my wife and me. We declined her offer of rent because Aimee was a gift to our family, and I suspect that we were a gift to her. Our own children were already in college or in their own new homes, so in a sense, Aimee filled a void for us.

Shortly after Aimee moved in, the television program American Idol started its current season. I know it is silly, but American Idol is a bit of a guilty pleasure for me. I was sitting in the living room, legs up on the couch.

"What are you watching?" a not timid voice piped up from behind me. It was Aimee; her friendly eyes almost laughing. She knew what I was watching, but she asked the question as a way to open a conversation. "American Idol," I chuckled. It had been a long day, and I was looking forward to this show after dinner.

"Can I watch with you?" She stepped into the living room and took a seat in the great armchair opposite the coffee table.

"Absolutely. You like American Idol?" I asked.

"Love it." We both laughed. After that night, we watched American Idol together every week. She was just like a daughter to me. She was a great gift to my wife and me. Aimee was as much family to us as our own children and, as it is a gift to help our own children, it was a gift to help Aimee and see her develop and grow. Today, she is very successful in her own life, and we were glad to help her.

I believe that family is a state of mind. Strong family relationships are good for everyone, a win-win. My wife tells me I am a very positive person. I truly do not have bad days. I cannot say that I know what depression is, at least not from experience.

I am very blessed with an abundance of family. Everyone in my family helps keep me happy and active. It is hard work raising children, but if you lead your children in the right direction and treat them well, they will in turn become the best gifts life and God can give.

In a Father's Day card, my eldest daughter Jennifer wrote, "You are a special father . . . and now even a grandfather of three! May the pieces of wisdom you taught and modeled for me be something I also pass on to my children." All boasting aside, I think it is wonderful that Jennifer saw my wisdom and attitude as something to emulate and teach her own children. I think she has learned the right way to raise children; her children are two little extra gifts in my life.

When we are dating in our youth, we often date people who absolutely not right for us, but I don't think most of us really figure out the type of person who is right for us until we get a little older, a little more mature. When I began to seek a proper mate, in God's timing I would say, I worked out what it was that would make a woman right for me. I met the woman, Sharon, I married, and I quickly figured it out.

We had the same values and interests. Miraculously, we both wanted four children (and we are both children from big families). When you get right down to it, matching principles and standards are the important factors. You could be as different as night and day, but that does not matter if you want the same things out of life.

We take care of each other. I provided for her and our children, and my wife raised our children wonderfully. And by another miraculous twist of fate, we did have exactly four children. She is a gift to me, and I to her. We are partners in this world, and we will be in the next. I am glad we were able to show our children what a good, stable home is.

There is a saying that "behind a man's success is a wonderful woman." My wife has been and will continue be a blessing in my life and the lives of our children. She sacrificed her job by staying at home to personally take care each child. She knew the value of being a stay-at-home Mom.

When I began to work as a young, inexperienced doctor, I had a number of misconceptions about the career I had ahead of me. I thought doctors were always successful—had huge mansions and drove big, fancy cars—although by themselves, they are not wrong, and they are fine when you can afford to have them. Well, I found out that this is not always true. By sheer good fortune, I was introduced to an older doctor took me under his wing and taught me some critical lessons in my life. He taught me that the first business of being a doctor was to provide care for the patient and that monetary success flowed only as a result of doing the first job to the best of one's abilities. He hired me to work in his medical center. I soon became enamored with the concept of one day having and owning a similar medical center of my own. I studied how my mentor's business worked at providing excellent health care services. I began to understand that in any endeavor, one must offer real benefits to receive real rewards. My vision began to form around a medical center whose ultimate success was predicated upon first giving something of value to those in need of it. I changed my original idea of a successful doctor from one who displays the trappings of success, into the one where giving valuable health care is the real indicator of any doctor's success. Doctors take an oath when we begin our careers. As I matured under my mentor, I found it good to reflect on what those oaths mean in the overall balance of my life. This practice gave me the perspective to see broader horizons, and subsequently, truer visions of what I saw my life could become.

CHAPTER FOUR
Vision

"Success often comes to those who have the aptitude to see way down the road." —Laing Burns Jr.

People often ask me why I chose to become a doctor. From a young age, my mother had a vision for each of her children—me and my two brothers and four sisters. My brothers were clearly going to be suited to the family business because they had the right temperament for it.

I suppose I was different. It was not necessarily my vision at first to become a doctor, but it was my mother's. She had a keen gift for reading people, especially her own children. Fortunately as a young man, I was wise enough to seek my mother's counsel. Although I was born and raised in my early years in Indonesia, I went to an American school located on the other side of the island; thanks to my parents' wisdom. I subsequently transferred to the Philippines for college and medical school. Following the medical school graduation, I moved to California and completed my Masters in Public Health at Loma Linda University.

My medical career led me to residency training in Maryland, and during that period, I met a doctor, who eventually became my mentor. I will call him Doctor Mentor. There were days when I stepped in to take care of his patients when he showed up late or not at all. He was pleased with my work and started to ask me about myself.

We discovered that we had many things in common, including graduating from Loma Linda University. I was new to the workforce and concerned about whether or not I would be able to face the day-to-day encounters with people that I might have to treat. I was not certain if I had the ability to develop a good physician-patient relationship. Did I possess the communication skills to do that? Did I have sufficient language skills to perform adequately?

Doctor Mentor had an amazing medical center. He was one of the forerunners in Urgent Care and other innovations in medicine. He was an excellent doctor; he had both a keen understanding of the practice of medicine as well as several innovative ideas. Well-liked by his patients, he was also a well-respected leader in the community. I was privileged to be asked to join his practice. That was a gift to me, and he was a gift to me because I was able to learn from him and to be mentored by him. I had an inkling that someday I wanted to have a medical center like his. His practice served as the model—the basis for my own vision of medical care.

I worked for Doctor Mentor for about four years and for much of that time, a dream was taking root in my mind. I believe a vision is something that one works toward for a long time—thinking, planning, and shaping and reshaping—as the vision grows clearer and better defined. Although the scope and shape of that vision was initially vague in my mind, it began to develop during this time. We all experience the desire to shape our own vision at some point in our lives, but it takes patience and hard work to actively pursue such a vision until it becomes a reality.

As time went on, the relationship between Doctor Mentor and me soured, changing from win-win into a win-lose relationship. Through the counsel of my family, I realized that the time had come for me to start my own practice.

At this time, my younger brother was starting out as a doctor in California. He was married and needed financial aid to see him through medical school, while I was single and doing very well financially working at Doctor Mentor's medical center. I told him, "You know what, Rio? I'm going to buy a house for you in California." So I bought my brother and his wife a house. I made the payments on it, and they stayed there.

My brother Rio had been a businessman and has a good sense for business practice and economic growth. I spoke to him about my emerging vision of establishing my own medical center. Both my mother and my brother supported my vision. Rio and I discussed my idea of opening my own medical practices on the phone one afternoon. I was home, so it must have been a Saturday. We were talking about my idea of opening up a practice. I was still sketchy on the details; I didn't know yet that I was going to open up a full medical center. The concept of a private practice was still lingering in my thoughts. In many ways, setting up a simple solo practice would be easier to achieve. I called him because he has a brilliant business mind. He told me, "Stephen, go for the medical center. You can do it."

I waffled a bit, although deep down I knew I was going to try. "I'm not sure. It is what I want to do, but is now the time?"

"Look, what you need to do is find a practice that is already active. That way, you do not have to start completely from scratch," said Rio.

He was absolutely right about that. "Yeah. I think I heard about a doctor who is planning to retire. I don't know much about him though."

Together, we found the practice run by an older doctor who was looking to retire. With love and support, my mother provided me with the seed money. Given the business minds of my family, my mother could have told me, "Stephen, I want to help you build up the practice, but I want 50 percent." She did not do this.

Without that financial gain, her support is still a win-win relationship because of the mother-son relationship. It is a gift to a mother to see her son become successful. When she reaches old age, I will be able to take care of her properly. Regardless, it is emotionally rewarding to be able to help a loved one, and it is a gift to have a parent who is able and willing to help. So you see, this is a win-win relationship in which there is no selfish gain.

In this same manner, my brother was a gift to me. He nurtured my vision of what my practice could become with his understanding of both business and medicine. He advised me to purchase the practice from the retiring doctor, and I did. There was only one problem: the practice was located in a small house, which could not be expanded under the zoning rules. These small walls could not contain my greater vision. However, the retiring doctor's practice provided me a foundation that could be used as a stepping stone for growth at another location, because the practice was thriving and had a good number of patients to carry over to a larger medical center.

To set up a medical practice definitely takes a vision. One can operate a single mom-and-pop office or develop and expand a medical center, where the focus is not practicing as individual physician but drawing patients to a group of health care providers. A medical center offers patients more comprehensive medical and health care, and that was the ultimate goal of my vision.

It was also clear to me that it would be wise to have my own building rather than renting an office space because I intended to be in medical practice for the long haul. By having my own property, I wouldn't have to pay rent increases. So my next goal was to find land suitable for building the medical center.

Once I had purchased the land from Mr. Carrigan, and the architect had completed his drawing, I needed to contact the construction company. I chose to have a design build or turnkey project. That, I believed, would reduce the stress and the anxiety of dealing with different contractors.

In determining the size of the building, I needed to find the balance between building the maximum size of structure allowed by the zoning regulations and a plan to construct the building in stages as the practice expanded and funds increased. The builder preferred to construct the largest building permitted by the zoning code. However, that would require a big loan up-front. Did we need to build extra space in the beginning when we only had one doctor and a few employees?

We decided to build the building in stages—starting at the front side, leaving room to add later to the back of the building. Once we were using all rooms on the first floor, we would complete the upstairs portion of the building. So we began with one physician and then added other primary care providers as well as specialists.

After operating the medical center successfully for almost fifteen years, we were approached by several potential buyers who wanted to purchase the assets of the medical center including the building. Only medical doctors can own a medical practice, but others can own the assets belonging to the practice. At least three corporations wanted to purchase the assets of the practice.

After two years, we agreed to sell to a company from Arizona. During the negotiations, I took to heart the advice from my brother Rio about the psychology of buying and selling a business. He told me that buyers tend to encourage sellers to expect a high price, but anticipate that sellers will become overconfident about the sale and slack off in performance, thus, decreasing the value of the business, and then the buyer will ultimately pay less. Following my brother's advice, I continued to work hard to remain profitable, putting the idea of possible sale out of my mind. The potential buyer periodically requested up-to-date financial reports. My brother told me a story of a successful practice in California that became a victim of negative psychology. The practice that was once the best and the most profitable showed a downstream in the performance and ultimately was sold for almost nothing.

As a result of following my brother's advice, I received an irresistible offer from the buyer. I sold the center but was asked to stay with the new company, working both as a doctor and a medical director. Thus, I received a significant amount of cash up front, and at the same time, I was compensated as a medical doctor with a higher salary than I was earning before the purchase.

The proceeds from the sale enabled me to pay off our household debts, and we became debt-free. The Bible tells us that we need to take care of our own household first then the community. In addition, the Scripture advises us the wisdom of being debt-free. Isn't it being debt-free the definition of being financially independent?

Several years later, the new owners were not able to operate the medical center profitably because they were in Arizona rather than Maryland. Eventually, the practice and the assets reverted to a group of us who were originally involved with the medical center.

At that time, we created a Limited Liability Corporation (LLC) to purchase back the assets at a much lower price than the Arizona group had paid. Each member of the LLC contributed a modest amount of money to pay the down payment, and then the LLC arranged a mortgage for the real estate and other assets. The physicians who were loyal to the original medical center were rewarded with ownership. They had been gifts to me. Today, all members of the LLC have an equal share in the medical center and equal limited liability.

"To have a vision is to be able to think forward, to plan ahead, and to be able to see the benefit to come in the future."

I knew then that Mr. Carrigan also owned the land next to the medical center. I could see the possible benefit of purchasing that land for future expansion. At the time, this property was leased to a family-style restaurant frequented by locals, nearby workers, and travelers. I mentioned to Mr. Carrigan my interest in purchasing that property from him if and when he was ready to sell. Letting him know of my interest ahead of time was a prudent way of planning.

It might be a visionary to let others know your interest.
"Planning ahead is a virtue."

He made it clear to me that he did not wish to sell the property at that time. However, approximately one year later, he called to let me know he was ready to sell if I still wanted to buy the land. My answer was an immediate yes. The purchase was finalized, and it was one of the best investments I ever made. The price was great, and even after arranging financing, the monthly payment was still less than the rent income from the restaurant. The restaurant had a twenty-year lease that guaranteed the financial stability of that property.

I later found out that the reason Mr. Carrigan wanted to sell the property to me was that, apparently, the owners of the restaurant had been calling him, asking to purchase the property. Instead of selling the lot to them, he sold it to me. I believe he did that because of our positive relationship.

"A positive relationship leads to more and better relationships, while a negative relationship terminates the relationship." "A positive relationship begets another positive relationship."

The Bible says that the love of money is the root of all evil. I do not mean to say that money is evil. People need it to survive in this world. Rather, I think the Bible is concerned with the intentions of our hearts. If your intent—your greatest desire and goal—is to earn a lot of money, then I believe you will fail. This is not the way to approach life.

"Everyone has a talent. If you take that talent and develop it, train yourself to do what you love, and work hard at what you do by putting your whole heart into your job, I do believe that the money will come."

"Money is a by-product, but should not be the object of our work."

Happiness is important. What is money if you are not happy with what you do? You cannot be a gift to others if you are unfulfilled because your heart is not in your work, and you are disappointed with your position in life.

The trick is to figure out your own talents or to have the wisdom to listen when someone points them out to you. My mother, with all her maternal intuition, discerned that medicine would be the right field for me. I listened to her and never really considered any other career; medicine was instilled in me from such an early age.

Children dream of a million different professions before they are ten—each dream wilder than its predecessor. They see themselves as a fireman extinguishing great flames, a dinosaur charging through the trees, a doctor saving lives, or a veterinarian taking care of puppies. These are the dreams of children. When you are a child, the entire world is open to you. It is full of endless possibilities.

I pursued that dream of being a doctor, and I know I made my mother happy by taking her excellent advice. She helped me develop in that direction. So it was very rewarding for her to see me pursue my vision. But a career is not just about your calling; the path must be good for you, too.

My younger brother Rio was a successful businessman. He was involved in exports and imports in Indonesia, and he fueled the success of the family business. He was very good at it. He knew all the rules of the business world; he had all the right contacts and connections. Even though Rio was the best and achieved financial success, the job was stressful, and he was very unhappy. He developed a painful stomach ulcer, which was his body's way of telling him that this career was wrong for him.

So he said, "No more! I want to go to America and go back to school." Following his heart, Rio moved to California and went to medical school. Fortunately, he still harbors that talent for business, which has given him great success in his medical career. Today, he is also doing some business in California; it's less stressful for him in moderation.

The important thing is that he pursued his vision, and it brought him happiness. His great business instincts are a gift. These instincts have often been a gift to me.

Other doctors in my area are impressed with my supposed talent in managing a medical center because they think I have an aptitude for business. They see me as both a good doctor and a good businessman. But they do not see the man behind the curtain—my brother who gives me great counsel in business and is a great gift to me.

Rio is an outstanding example of how to be a gift to others. To be a gift to others, you must have vision, and you must also be a gift to yourself. I find my purpose in being a gift to my wife, my children, my family, my friends, my coworkers, and everyone around me. My vision gives me something toward which to work—a goal. I know that I am on the right path and that makes me happy. I support myself in order to support my family.

Rio changed career paths because business made him sick in body and spirit. He could not be a gift to others because when he was pursuing business, simply making money, he was not taking care of himself. It is not selfish to want to be happy and to take care of yourself. We must love and take care of ourselves before we can love and take care of others.

I am a happy man. I can honestly say that I have never been depressed. There are transient moments of grief, but by their very nature, they pass. If you are happy in the field you have chosen and work hard, the money you need to support yourself and your family will come to you. Financial success is a by-product of working hard at what you love.

Another doctor once asked me, "Why are you so happy?" I thought about this for a moment, but could not produce a good answer. I told him, "Well, I don't know. That's just how I am. I'm happy—it's true. No matter what happens, I'm still happy." Happiness is a frame of mind. It is a mindset that you bring to your approach to life and all the things you do. My life here on earth is a gift from God. You only get one chance at life, so you have to do your best while you are here. We will all die one day, but we cannot know when that will happen. So while you are alive, you must live and make the most of the gift of life by being a gift to others.

In a sense, what is best for you is what is best for others. You must be your best self, so you can be a gift to others. It is a stewardship of the self. You can't think "me, me, me." That said, you do have to take care of yourself, do what is right for your own well-being in order to take care of others. That is how I approach relationships with my family, my children, and all others in my life. The term self-centered has a negative connotation, but it is not a completely negative concept. It is a positive thing to take care of oneself.

There is a darker side to this though. What if there is a father who is a successful man in his business, but who craves money?

He desires to be more successful at work, and he thinks of nothing else. He provides for his family financially, but they suffer because the emotional relationships are strained. How can he be there for his family if he spends all his time and thoughts on his career? The family falls apart. This businessman's wife might leave him, and his children will likely get into trouble.

"Success is a balance. Work hard, but work smart."

This means we have to manage our time wisely. I have four children. They are all in their twenties now, but when they were younger, I made the effort to attend their various activities, sporting events, recitals, and birthday parties. I think it is important to play a role in the lives of your children. Children, by definition, are new to this world and need guidance. They need the support of their parents. If you do not build healthy relationships with them, later in life they will resent you because they have suffered.

That is what is really important to me. I think you can measure your success by your children's happiness. Are you available for your children? What are their interests? Take the time to get involved. That is true success for you and being there for your children will help them succeed later in life.

It is a key to build a strong relationship with each child early on. If you have devoted time to your children from the beginning, they will later come to you for advice and counsel. You will be able to help them construct a vision for their own future. That is what my mother did for me. So you see, she was a gift to me, and thus, allowed me to become a gift to my children.

I was a new doctor working in a medical center in Maryland. Young, green, and still wet behind the ears, I naturally thought I knew it all. My life was all ahead of me, and I was excited for it to begin. The facilities I worked in were excellent—the environment was stimulating, and the people were top-notch. Then a friend completely surprised me. One day she, call her LP, came to me saying she was leaving not just the city or state, but the country. She was giving up her life to devote it

35

to helping others on a missionary ship designed to cruise the world, stopping to render aid and Christian support to those devastated by disasters, wars, disease, and famine. I couldn't understand it at first. Why would such a lovely, young, and talented woman at the very beginning of her career throw it away for such work? Even as she left and continued to write to me, I couldn't fully grasp the reasoning behind her actions. For a good while, I received letters and news clips from around the world as her ship traveled from hot spot to hot spot across the vast oceans. Eventually, it dawned on me that maybe she was not throwing her career away. I began to understand that maybe her decision wasn't to waste her life but was merely the beginning of a more important career: to do God's work. I finally revised my perspective and arrived at a place where I could see that my unformed, immature ideas of success were not her idea of success. I understood more about how much I didn't understand, which, some say, is the beginning of wisdom. I began to put more faith in God and things that were not crystal clear to my limited intellect. My spirit was beginning to come alive, to have faith, and beginning to grow up.

CHAPTER FIVE
Wisdom

"It is a characteristic of wisdom not to do desperate things."
—Henry David Thoreau

I do not claim to be a wise individual, but in my lifetime, I have learned a few things about wisdom, and I have also known a few very wise people.

Through them and through my own life experiences, I think I have learned how wisdom pertains to the gift of our existence and how we can contribute to each other's lives as gifts.

Andre Gide said, "Believe those who are seeking the truth; doubt those who find it." Follow the path of those who are seeking that truth, and you might be following their wisdom. But what is wisdom? The Princeton dictionary defines wisdom as "accumulated knowledge or erudition or enlightenment." I like that—"accumulated knowledge." I think that fits exactly what I am trying to say here.

As a child grows, he accrues information about his world. He learns that fire burns and that crayons make colors on paper (or walls, if he is a naughty boy). As a teenager, he must rely on that accumulated knowledge to see that his parents are trying to impart advice for his own good. The obvious problem is that teenagers are rarely wise individuals.

Wisdom comes from many sources. It comes as advice from family members, from the parents, from the siblings, or from the children. It also may come from reading and from conversation among a group of people.

But the best source of wisdom is the Bible. James 1:5 says, "If any of you lacks wisdom, he should ask God, who gives generously to all without finding fault, and it will be given to him." Proverbs 2:6 says, "For the Lord gives wisdom, and from his mouth come knowledge and understanding."

Wisdom, wise counsel, is particularly important in times of trouble. Knowing when to accept the advice of a trusted person in your life can be your saving grace. I could not have achieved what I have today if I had not had the wisdom to accept the counsel of those close to me, especially my mother. I understood that she knew what she was talking about, and I knew she would be pleased and proud when I put her advice to good use.

Mothers carry an inherent wisdom waiting in great stores for the chance to be cast on the ears of hopefully listening children.

In my early twenties, I started dating a beautiful lady. She turned heads everywhere she went, and when she walked in front of me, men actually grabbed at her. But when I introduced her to my mother, my mother began to cry. She drew me aside later and told me, "Stephen, she's not the right person for you. If you stay with her, you will be miserable in the future."

In my immaturity, I was blind to any imperfections in this gorgeous young woman. My mother shocked me, but I respected her wisdom ultimately. It was rather like being doused with a bucket of cold water. But mothers carry a wisdom gained with age and are only too happy to bestow it on their children. My mother was emotionally wounded by my choice of girlfriend, and I had a difficult time seeing her so sad. I heeded her advice and broke up with my girlfriend.

On reflection, I'm glad I did not marry her. Although I couldn't see it at the time, we were not right for each other; we were completely different people. But my mother, in her wisdom, could see that, and although I might not have been wise in dating that girl, I did recognize the wisdom in seeking counsel.

If you are involved in healthy win-win relationships with members of your family, you would not be remiss in seeking or taking their counsel when your life is at a crossroads, and you are not sure how to proceed. Sometimes you will find that those who love you know you better than you know yourself, and through that knowledge, can aid your efforts to find the right path. The support of family is a blessing not to be taken lightly. They will keep you afloat even when you fail in your endeavors.

When I was starting out with my medical practice, I remember my mother actually telling me, "Stephen, it is okay if you fail. We learn from our mistakes." I must admit that I was a little alarmed when I heard the same thing from my brother. Certainly, I wasn't going to fail as miserably as they seemed to think I might. They did not actually think I was going to fail; they were just trying to reassure a first time entrepreneur.

As I've said, my brother Rio helped me find the right place to start my practice. One day, while I was driving and we were stopped at a red light, he turned to me. He gave my shoulder a reassuring squeeze.

"Stephen, remember to not take yourself and your business too seriously," he told me.

"What do you mean?" I cast him a quick glance before returning my attention to the red light. Cars were zooming across our fields of vision.

"I mean that you should know that it is okay to fail."

I laughed at this somewhat nervously. How could I be getting this from all sides? What kind of pearls of wisdom should I take away from these comments about failure?

"Mom told me that last week. Do you guys know something that I don't?" Rio laughed at that.

"We don't want you to put too much pressure on yourself. You are a doctor first, a businessman second. Even if this doesn't pan out, you will always have medicine on its own. So relax."

The light changed to green. I was still looking at Rio. The car behind us honked and brought me back to attention. I turned left, and we found the perfect location for my medical center on that next street.

Looking back on this moment with my brother, I am reminded of the importance of taking counsel from family members. It is wise not take oneself too seriously. Rio was right. His wisdom and patience were gifts to me. In turn, I have tried my best to be a gift to him and to my mother. The reciprocity in these moments and in relationships is what fuels my understanding of gifts. Wisdom is a gift. It strikes me that the wisdom of counsel is necessary in times of trouble.

"There are obviously many kinds of wisdom, but knowing when to accept the advice of a trusted person in your life can be your saving grace."

I could not have made it to where I am today if I had not had the wisdom to accept the counsel of those close to me. Advice came from several corners of my life and at various stages of the journey. I would not say that I am a wise soul, but I understood that my mother knew what she was talking about. Her advice would benefit me, and I knew she would take it with personal pride when I put her advice to good use.

If you get sick, you go to the doctor. You seek the advice of a trained medical professional. If the doctor prescribes medicine, you take it because, in our culture, we trust doctors and their training. That's the conventional wisdom. The same wisdom must be applied to all areas of life to ensure mental and spiritual well-being. As a teenager, I was aimless with little ambition. My parents sent me to the "reform" school to change my attitude and my outlook. But my mother also forced me to see the path that was right for me. I took the prescription; I went to medical school.

Wisdom involves knowing what is right for the individual. No two people are alike. What is good for one person is not necessarily good for everyone else. Only by knowing yourself and your talents can you find the right path for yourself. That path will hopefully lead you to a happy place full of gifts. It is wise to acknowledge the gifts in your life, whether that means family, friends, or a good career. Appreciation is a key element of wisdom.

> *"As we grow older and gain more experience in life, we have more gifts given to us."*

We are all born with talents and abilities. It is sometimes hard to recognize them because we have never been without them. How do we open our eyes to see ourselves more objectively, soberly in the context of the world? It is important to recognize life's hierarchy. To a rich young man, having money is something he might always have had. He cannot appreciate it because he has never been without.

This is true of all our gifts. It sometimes is difficult to see what they are—be it an ability to be a good friend, to play basketball, or to sing. But we must develop wisdom to make the use of our natural born gifts.

It's important for others to see that we have used our inherited gifts wisely. If our friends, family, coworkers, or community do not recognize us as gifts to them, then we are ineffective. There are times when we will be misinterpreted, misread, lied about, or misunderstood. The failure of others to recognize and acknowledge our gifts is one of life's most painful problems.

What do you do when you are not seen as a gift to people? What if people do not consider you a good friend, a good worker, a good husband or wife, or a good father or mother? If your value is not acknowledged, you have to take the higher ground and recognize that being a gift can mean leaving the situation.

This is not abandonment, neglect, or dereliction of duty in work or school. It simply means that you must realize you are actually damaging yourself and the person or people who do not recognize you for who you are by staying in the relationship with them. Therefore, you must be a bigger gift and quit the job or separate from your spouse. And if there is a big problem, possibly a problem that you yourself have made, you must leave the community. This is "being a gift" to the people around you that do not recognize you. Hard to swallow, but true.

We all fail. We all sin. We all fall short every day, every week, and every year. Becoming religious does not mitigate this. We still are incapable of living up to our desire to be a gift all the time. This is where seeing yourself and your life as a gift becomes the most crucial. If we are to be gifts to others, the worst thing we can do is attempt to cover up our sins, our failures. Why is this so? Because the fact is, everyone else on the planet fails. It is what we do with our failures that count.

Wisdom covers a lot of ground and takes many forms. It is important to recognize wise counsel from friends and family. Little pearls of wisdom can be found in the most mundane of moments—in our failures as well as our success stories—and these pearls can be passed on to our children, friends, and loved ones.

It was my first brand-new automobile. I was in car heaven. Here was a young doctor with his American dream car—a gold V8 Pontiac Firebird. It made a deep, aggressive rumble from its dual exhaust when you pressed on the gas. The interior smelled of new leather and the tires were wider than my twin hand span. I had just picked it up from the dealership and headed for the interstate highway. Each upshift of the gears brought a wider grin to my boyish face. High speed built up in a matter of seconds. The on-ramp included a sharp right turn without much an acceleration lane. Too late, the newness of the driving experience got the best of me, and without knowing it, I was doing autobahn speeds as I approached the curve. I was going way too fast for my experience—my Vespa scooter never ever went this fast. I slammed on the brakes and tried desperately to slow down, but I was already in the apex of the turn. The brakes broke the wide tires loose. I was in a full four-wheel drift at triple digits heading into a high-speed rush hour and in a car I had driven all of ten blocks from the dealer. The gold Firebird spun around 360 degrees. My life flashed in front of my eyes along with the sight of the cars in the neighboring lanes. I was certain I was going to die. To my surprise, the Firebird stopped spinning and slowed, pointed in the right direction in the middle of the slow lane. I gunned the engine and brought her up to a safe, minimum speed, although my heart was hammering at full speed. I decided then and there that next time, I would work my way to driving my Firebird at any kind of speed. I was willing to drive fast, but I hadn't experienced directing this effort in a safe manner. I was alive because my guardian angel made a space for me in that packed, rush-hour traffic. I thanked my Maker for another precious gift: my life.

CHAPTER SIX
Effort

This might sound obvious or even trite, but it is important to do your best and actively attempt to be your best in all aspects of life. Being in tip-top shape makes it easier for you to be a gift to others and to receive their gifts. I find that I am more aware and able to work efficiently and effectively if I go into the office every morning with the right attitude. Mental clarity contributes greatly to this.

Being fully present to the task in front of you is critical to giving it your best effort. Think of a tennis match. To be a good and challenging tennis opponent, you must first take care of yourself. If you are healthy and ready to play, you will give your opponent a better match.

Several years ago, a patient came to me with severe abdominal pain. I could see that she was going to need more help than I could offer as a general practice family doctor. So I referred her to a gastroenterology (GI) specialist who was able to treat her effectively for the small benign tumors that she had, and now she is happy and healthy. I received thank-you from both the patient and her other doctor. She told me that I had "saved her life."

That GI specialist called me up to ask, "How did you know?" Now I did not know that she had tumors, but I suspected as much. Without my smugness, I told him that it was a gift of experience and education. I was able to put together all of the symptoms, the laboratory findings, and the important variable of age. I went into the office that day ready to take care of my patients, supported by those two key tools in the arsenal of a professional experience and education. I was at my best and thankful for these gifts.

In this case, my experience and education enabled me to be a gift. But it was also a gift to me in return because it showed me how far my experience and education could take me. It is emotionally rewarding to help someone in this way. As you can tell, I was a gift to this patient. Being a gift in this way is simple: just approach life with the desire to be your best.

"This is not a matter of being successful in your chosen career or in personal matters, but rather all about opening yourself up to be a gift to those around you."

Proverbs 10:4 sum it up quite well, "Lazy hands make a man poor, but diligent hands bring wealth." I believe the term "wealth" here encompasses more than material wealth. I believe this proverb focuses us on our intent and effort.

I go to work every day intending to help people; I do not go to my office with a primary goal of making money. We should all be diligent in our day-to-day lives, endeavoring to be the best we can be with the intention of making the world better for everyone. I know that sounds rather naïve, but there are many people who live by this creed, and they are happy regardless of financial success.

Does it do you any good to relentlessly pursue money? No. You will be miserable. I've heard stories of men who worked on Wall Street, right there in the bull pen, who developed ulcers and cancerous tumors. Their never-ending, stressful desire for money literally made them sick.

My own brother experienced this. He was a businessman. The stress he experienced with his work gave him an ulcer, and he eventually changed his career. He chose a less stressful, albeit lower-paying path, and now he is much happier and healthier as a result.

That is, of course, an extreme example, but I think many people have similar experiences. God gives everyone a talent. You might have several talents—those things that actually make you happy; those little things you are truly good at doing. Why not put in the effort and pursue them? What good is it to work hard at something that does not bring joy to your life?

I repeatedly remind and tell my children, "Work hard. Strive to do what you love and do not be lazy about it. If you do your best, the money will follow." Life is too short to spend inordinate amounts of time doing things that do not make you happy.

Being a gift to yourself is not just about exploring your talents and developing them. You must be a steward of your own well-being. Too much unhappiness or stress can have frightful effects on the body. Regardless of your income, you can eat well and take care of yourself. For example, did you know it is cheaper to buy raw vegetables than it is to buy frozen foods or packaged snacks?

Also, healthy habits such as walking and bicycling are free or low cost. I find that walking is good for both the body and the soul. Like prayer and meditation, walking gives you time to reflect on your day and think about the future. It provides your mind time to process and consider events in your life. Too often in these modern times, the television, the Internet, and video games distract us. The mind is always working to process so many stimuli. It's healthy to take a break and let your mind rest.

"Taking care of your body and mind is a gift to yourself. It allows for longevity and sensible forethought. You cannot be a gift to others unless you are happy and healthy."

Inner joy is an important step to living well. The Bible tells us: "Love thy neighbor as thyself." We tend to forget the "as thyself " aspect of this command. It is deemed selfish to love oneself in Western tradition.

But it is not selfish to take care of yourself because you cannot take care of your children and support your family if you are not also taking care of yourself. If you come down with a cold because you have been overlooking your own well-being, you will not be able to go to work and make the money needed to provide for your family. Where is the sense in that? That is a lose-lose situation.

Be 100 percent present in every situation. Be aware of your thoughts and be present in that meeting, on that date, or at that baseball game with your son. Once the task is accomplished, you will be able to properly reflect on those moments. The person with whom you've just interacted will remember that you concentrated fully on him or her and know that you care.

This is important both in business and in personal life. You make yourself a gift to others simply by being there and listening. No one likes the person who only half listens and replies with "Uh-huhs" and "Yeahs." Interact with something more than your computer, and you will feel fulfilled.

"To be successful is to be focused."

Successful men and women share one common trait: they are focused on what they are doing. I like the idea of focusing on one patient at a time as I am working as a physician. I advise my children and other young people—and to encourage them—to keep their mind on the task or person at hand to be successful.

Being 100 percent present does not mean being perfect. No one is perfect. We improve by learning from our mistakes.

So when you are on a date, focus on that person; do not take a business call. That is a severe mistake, and your date will not likely forgive you for it. By the same token, do not parade your "goodness." That is not being a gift to others. Help someone or do something with someone because you genuinely want to do so. Demonstrate your integrity by your actions.

Sometimes others do not recognize us as being gifts. Once you realize this situation, you should take the higher ground and recognize that the best way to be a gift in that situation is to leave it. This is not condoning dereliction of duty in work or school. It simply means that you must realize you are actually doing damage to yourself and to the person or people who do not recognize you for who you are by staying in the relationship with them.

It is best in this situation to quit the job. This is how you can be a gift to the people around you that do not recognize your efforts. Hard to swallow, but it is true. We need to do our best in whatever we do, for doing our best is a sign of obedience to God. God has given each person certain talents. As we do our best, we are being obedient in using those talents wisely. However, we also need to learn how to be content with what we have.

My first daughter Jennifer and her husband Christian live in small duplex house in southern California. The house has two bedrooms and one bathroom. It measures slightly less than one thousand square feet. However, it has nice front yard and an adequate backyard. They now have two little sons and two daughters.

I am so glad to see them so content with they have. While their home is small, they are not sorry; they are happy with what they have. They frequently invite friends and neighbors to their house. They have wonderful fellowship with the members of their church. Being content is a gift, and they have it. There is nothing wrong, however, if one day they want to move to a bigger house as their family grows.

"It is not about what we are doing. It is about what God wants us to do, and do it best for him."

I loved rock 'n' roll during my teenage years. It was alive. It was the music of my times, and we all danced to it with complete abandon. We listened to it in our bedrooms and sang it in our bathrooms, our cars, and with our friends. It was the background of our lives; the soundtrack of our existence. Yet one thing about rock 'n' roll troubled me greatly after having listened to it for a number of years. My favorite singers, guitar players, and even drummers began to check out at an unbelievable rate. My generation's stars were dying so quickly. It seemed like every few months there was yet another death. Sure, one might say it was the sign of the times: lots of unacceptable activities occurred within the context of sometimes strange and bizarre lifestyles. But I am saddened beyond the loss of such musical genius like Jim Morrison, Jimi Hendrix, Keith Moon, and many more. I feel that the talents these people possessed were gifts from God. And as such, they had a responsibility to nurture their gifts, to preserve them and even to bring those gifts to a higher level, if possible. We all have gifts given to us from above. Some get more than others to begin with, yet all can learn to receive more through giving more of themselves. It is a responsibility we all must acknowledge. If we are given gifts, then we must do our utmost to care for them to the best of our abilities. Caring for and developing our gifts is a kind of gift in itself.

CHAPTER SEVEN
Stewardship

Another important gift is the gift of financial stewardship. Although money is not everything in life, it is still important. God gives man wealth and possessions to enjoy. But if money is all that you love, then you are likely to have a very unhappy and unfulfilling life. Nevertheless, money is still important.

Money is the number one subject addressed in the Bible. In this modern world, we need money to live. That is just how it works. But we need to remember that God gives man wealth and possessions to enjoy. If money is all that you love, then you are likely to live a very unhappy and unfulfilling life.

As a business owner, I strive to be careful with finances and to watch over my medical center with a keen eye. It is a disservice to your business to squander money in a frivolous manner. Doctor Mentor taught me this much. He was a great doctor and likable person—just a bad businessman. He was always looking for ways to make more money.

The saying goes that if it looks too good to be true, it probably is. I remember that Doctor Mentor made some very bad investment choices, and he lost a lot of money every year because of that. Too often, he invested his money in searching for gold even in this day and age. If you told him there was gold to be found in the Appalachian Mountains, he would give you the money to go and find it for him. The next year it would be silver, and he would again give scam artists his hard-earned money.

Doctor Mentor was a brilliant doctor. An innovator, he created an urgent care center. It made me sad to see him squandering his money on bad investments, so I confronted him one day. We met in his office. I asked him how much money he had invested that year in one of those treasure-hunting scams. He told me, and it was a large sum.

"Doctor Mentor," I said, "you never seem to get good returns on these investments. Why don't you invest in your practice instead?" I suggested that he use his money to slowly purchase the building. However, he ignored my advice and continued to lose a lot of money over the next several years. If he had invested all that money over a period in his own practice, Doctor Mentor would have owned the building rather than renting the space.

There is a lesson in this. Do not waste your money on what are clearly poor investments. If you are unsure how best to manage your money, seek professional assistance. I get advice from my brothers who have keen business minds. I am not above seeking advice in areas where I have less expertise. In fact, it is wise to request advice from those who know more than we do.

Those who operate successful businesses must balance their budgets. We need to control our expenses and increase our income proportionately. We cannot spend what we do not have. We need to do our best to work hard to be profitable.

During an internship in my first years as a doctor, I had a great mentor. He was our attending physician, and I idolized him. He was successful and intelligent, a good role model, an example for us. I remember saying one day, "Gee, you're so successful. You must make lots of money."

You know what he said to me? "Stephen, right now you're just an intern. Don't worry about money right now. Instead, focus on learning as much as you can. If you do your best and work hard, the money will come later." I was taken aback. That was an answer grounded in reality, and it made me think hard about my situation. I followed his advice, and he was right.

Financial stewardship also involves vision. It is about looking to the long term. We all have to retire someday, and we cannot do it if we have nothing set aside.

My brother Rio advised me to pursue a three-stage strategy for building my medical center. I am thankful every day for this. Trying to build such a large structure at once would have been financial disaster, which is why many doctors treat patients well, but fail in creating a medical practice. We, doctors, are generally not the best businessmen.

A medical center such as mine requires patience. Constructing a building in stages is part of exercising patience. A friend of mine once said to me, "Wow Stephen! I have been here for years, and I never could have done what you are doing." I don't think that is entirely true. He could have constructed a medical center if he had the vision to do so and the patience to see his dream through to completion.

To be financially successful, it is important to look to the long term and maintain your initial good intentions. We all start out with good intentions. As people become successful in their chosen fields, they sometimes lose sight of their initial plans.

The love of money is the root of all evil. Idolatry plays a large part in this. When your business grows larger, you make a lot of money, and then you become selfish. Making money an idol leads to greed and abuse of power.

We need to distinguish between earning money to meet our needs versus loving money itself and always wanting more. Don't become a slave to the money you've earned. It is okay to have money and be financially secure, but making money shouldn't be your primary goal.

Oftentimes, the more money people make, the more they seem to need to spend. If your salary increases by $10,000 more a year, it does not mean you need to spend $10,000 more a year. It is smarter to save for the future or invest in a property.

I have heard the question "How much money do you need to be happy?" I think that money is irrelevant to happiness. Obviously, we need money to survive in the Western world and other developed countries, but money does not measure happiness—or rather it shouldn't measure happiness. If your bank statement is your measuring stick for happiness, I think you need to adjust your perspective.

Credit cards are another modern invention that often adversely affects the way people think about money. Your credit limit is not a line of free money. It is financially prudent to only spend as much with your card as you can feasibly pay off at the end of the month. This can be a good way to build credit for more important things in the future—such as a house or a car—but many Americans quickly get into trouble with this and build up debts that they cannot possibly pay.

To use credit cards wisely is a virtue. Use them to your advantage. You can delay payment for something you purchase for few weeks, while your money earns interest. However, you can put yourself in a dangerous position if you cannot pay off the whole balance you have charged on your card before the next billing cycle. Paying the high interest rates most credit cards charge can greatly increase your debt and the length of time it will take you to pay it off.

"Financial stewardship is about prudence."

How can you take care of your family if you do not make good choices with your money? You do not need big cars and designer clothing to be happy and take care of your family. It is a gift to your family to be sensible with your money. It is also a gift to you.

I have tried to teach my children about the importance of good financial stewardship, but at the same time, I warn them that making money an idol is a bad thing. It is okay to make money, but do not let finances control your life.

"Money should not be the primary goal."

"Making money should not come with greed."

"Money is the result, is the by-product, is the end result of what we do best."

"Making money comes with contentment."

"Money will follow."

A life story of a close friend of mine was told that he started a business on a shoestring. In few years, he had more than two dozen employees. His business was booming, and he could be called a certified small-business success. He moved his wife and children into a big, custom-built home with a huge backyard and sent his kids to top private schools. As the years went by, his wife complained about his work habits. They were still in what could be termed "early business survival mode," and she wanted him to slow down and smell the roses. He refused to slow down from working his weekdays, weeknights, and weekends' schedule. In short, he had become a total workaholic. Success had become addictive. His wife became tired of being ignored, rejected, lonely, and alone. She, a beautiful woman, soon attracted ardent admirers. Soon she was involved in an affair. When my friend discovered this, he was devastated. In great pain, he tried to throw himself into his work, but it was the wrong decision. He was in a state of constant pain, as he truly was in love with his wife. He soon began to lash out unthinkingly and pick blind fights with everyone at the office—employees, partners, and even clients. He soon wound up in court and lost everything.

So in his rush to make more and more money, he lost everything. His lost his family, his business, and for a brief period, even his sanity. Today, my friend is a completely changed man. He now measures each action that he is contemplating in terms of how it will affect the balance in his life. Money has a place, but so does love. He has learned through his mistakes that the gifts he is given—be it business success or personal relationships—must be cared for with a careful, thoughtful prudence. If my friend was given a chance to do it all again, I know that he would have acted in a totally different manner—and that his business and family would be with his still. He learned that gifts may be given, but how we balance and care for them is a serious responsibility.

CHAPTER EIGHT

Success

It is not selfish to be a gift to yourself. In a tennis match, you have to be a good player in order to make the game fun for the other player. If you have not taken good care of yourself by practicing, eating a good breakfast, and obtaining the proper equipment, you will not be fit to play, and the match will be rather one-sided. That is no fun for anyone.

Would you consider it selfish to eat and clothe yourself? I doubt it. You must be a gift to yourself before you can be a gift to others. Personal success is not the problem; it's what we do with our success that matters.

Some view success in terms of what money can buy—a big house, fancy cars, toys such as boats and planes. There is nothing wrong with having these nice things if we can use them to benefit other people, too.

Possessions can help develop win-win relationships. Do material things really matter when it comes to making you happy? I think instead one should focus on a good job, a family, and friends. Balancing personal and professional lives is the key to success. It's about time management and good stewardship of your finances.

Do you dream of success because you want to be the best you can be? Or is success a matter of financial gain? How you answer those questions will determine whether or not you are likely to be happy.

I have a friend who ran a very successful company. He recently sold it for quite a lot of money. As the steward of this company, he set aside 5 percent of the yearly income for charitable contributions.

Now you might be thinking, "Sure, whatever. He makes a lot of money, so what does it matter? I can't afford to do that." Not so, and I am not necessarily advocating that you go out and donate 5 percent of your yearly income. But my friend has been doing this from the very beginning of his career. Before he was a rich businessman, he was donating a portion of his income every year to charities. He now encourages his employees and children to do the same.

My friend's children grew up understanding the value of helping others. He raised them to recognize that helping others is a part of success. He is a gift to others, and his business was a gift to him. Again, I am not advocating that you necessarily do the same with your income, but the point is to be a gift to others with the gifts that God has given you. Use your talents in a way that is beneficial to others.

There are many ways to do this. My friend chose to make charitable contributions. You could choose to attend your child's ballet recitals or assist at a homeless shelter. Find a way to be a gift to others that is right for you.

I think giving to others is a measure of our success. If you measure your success by the good you do in the world rather than by the amount of money you make, you will be a happy person. I firmly believe that.

Looking back on your life in old age, you want to see that it has been composed of goodness and happiness. If you spent your life struggling simply to gain monetary success, do you think you will have experienced a full measure of the blessings of family life and friendship? That might be the case for a lucky few, but I think your elderly lips will be fraught with smiles and laughter if you have instead chosen to work at what you love and to surround yourself with good friends, family, and hobbies.

"Happiness means success because it means achieving a balance between family and career, including both work and play in your life."

A few years ago, I noticed that one of my employees was not performing as well as her coworkers. She and her coworkers choose their own hours; they operate on a clock-in/clock-out basis. As a result, it is easy to evaluate their performance. This particular employee was not logging nearly as many hours as the others.

Now I am not a believer in firing people. Nine times out of ten, there will be a better solution. It just requires time and dedication to find that better solution. So we sat down in my office to discuss her evaluation. I hoped that this would give us a chance to find the root problem affecting her work. Sometimes there are extenuating circumstances leading to low performance at work.

I presented her with a comparison of her hours versus her coworkers' hours. Now ideally, an employee is expected to produce a certain amount of work in a year. Based purely on performance, I explained to her that I could not give her a raise, which she understood. She did not expect one.

I wanted to understand her situation. I said, "Now the bottom line is this, I want to ask you, are you happy here? If you are not, then by all means, it is okay to look for another job. You know I will give you an excellent recommendation because we both know that you are a very smart person. There is nothing wrong with changing jobs, and there is certainly nothing wrong with your leaving because you are not happy here. Let me ask you this, okay? Do you really want to do what you are supposed to do? Or is there something else you would like to do? Would you rather be a nurse or a technician? If you do not enjoy your job, then you should make a change. You should do what makes you happy."

"Actually, I like what I'm doing. I get satisfaction from this job," she said. This surprised me. I was concerned for her well-being and how it had affected her work. I truly believe that you have to enjoy what you are doing to be successful. There is no incentive to work hard if you do not love your job, so I gave her a choice. She could stay if she really wanted to, or she could move on to pursue something else. It was a friendly, concerned ultimatum. She decided to stay.

After that meeting, the difference in her work was like day and night. This employee turned a corner and completely changed her attitude. She began to work harder. I think our meeting helped her realize that type of work she was doing was the right career for her. She still works for me, and she is great at what she does. She is a valuable asset to the medical center.

I think I helped her reevaluate her vision. She came to a new understanding about happiness. As you walk along your career path, your plan or vision for your future sometimes gets cloudy. When this happens, it is easy to lose your way and settle for a career that makes you unhappy.

I think many people lose sight of their vision when they measure success in terms of money. It is like a corporate ladder. Why keep climbing ladders toward a position that does not make you happy when you can start over on a different ladder that will lead to a job you'll really love? Sure, it will take time and effort to begin climbing the ladder that will lead to your desired career, but the hard work is worth it if you measure success in terms of happiness.

Greed is insatiable. If you abandon your vision in favor of money, then you will not be happy because you will always need more. Padding your pocketbook at the expense of your happiness might make you rich, but you will also be miserable.

"Success is measured by how you live your life and what you gain for living it in that way."

Look at the case of renowned stockbroker who is going to jail for the rest of his life. He achieved his life's ambition: money and power. He is a gift to no one. His means of obtaining success was theft, and we are not talking about the Robin Hood notion of theft in which one steals from the rich to give to the poor. No, that stockbroker stole from the rich and the poor to pad his own coffers. His family is now broken. What has he taught his children? That money is the key to happiness? How unfortunate. It is not my place to pass judgment, but his actions have resulted in legal judgments as well as great pain for those he stole from.

In the Western world, success is often measured by money and accomplishments. But that is not the only rubric. If success means happiness, then find the path to happiness, and success will follow. Be a gift to others.

That stockbroker was not a gift to anyone. In turn, the people he robbed were not gifts to him either. No one wins in this situation.

Instead of seeking only a financial return, focus on your talents. What are your talents? What do you have a gift for? I think you will find that, oftentimes, developing your talents will lead you to a happy career. God gives each person on this planet a talent. Some people get two or three talents, but they are not blessed unless they utilize these talents and develop them.

If you follow your talents to your life's work, you will experience contentment leading to happiness in other avenues of life. My mother was right to steer me in the direction of medicine because it is what makes me happy. If you unfortunately do not have the privilege of having a blessed mother, you may have another family member or even close friend who can give you sound advice. The point is that there may be someone in your life that could be gift to you.

I find great joy in being able to help people. If you work hard and are happy doing what you do, you will find that the money comes on its own. Employers like to reward hard work and good ethics.

"Part of being successful is knowing how to balance your professional and personal lives."

Your goal should be a balanced life.

This is a lot easier to do if your job makes you happy because you do not bring grief from the office to your family. Parents who are unhappy in their jobs tend to be less tolerant of their children's ups and downs and are more likely to snap at their children, which is sad. This leads to fighting in the home, which produces a bad environment for children.

Success at home can be very difficult, and it sometimes takes extreme patience and forbearance to keep the atmosphere civil. Sometimes success seems impossible, and the parents divorce. When you think about it, divorce is a better option than constant shouting and fighting in front of children.

There is an old English proverb that says, "A stumble may prevent a fall." Your saving grace on the road to success could be that little setback. Of course, a little setback could mean a big lifestyle change, such as a divorce, but it is better in the long run.

A setback could mean facing failure. There is nothing wrong with failing once in a while. No one is perfect, and no one is going to succeed 100 percent of the time. Bill Gates once said, "Success is a lousy teacher. It seduces smart people into thinking they can't lose."

Too much success sets you up for a serious blow to the ego. When you finally do fail, it is going to be a very painful experience. For example, in tennis, oftentimes, if I win the first set, I get overconfident. When this happens, I generally lose the second set. When you become overconfident, you can get sloppy. Success is about consistency and balance. Do not lose faith if you make a mistake. Failing is an important learning process.

This also holds true on the corporate ladder. Say, for example, you are a successful salesman on track to become a manager. This is great if you want to be in that line of work for the rest of your life. But you must ask yourself, "Is this what I really want?" If your real desire is to be a graphic designer or a lawyer, it is better to go back to school and start all over again than to continue on your current path.

There can be setbacks, especially if you are the breadwinner for your family. On the face of it, a career change might not seem financially feasible. But there are always ways around this. Your spouse could get a job, and you might be eligible for a scholarship for your education.

My brother Rio was already married when he decided to switch careers. He went to medical school, but I assisted his family by purchasing a house for them. There is always a way to achieve your dreams. It may take a lot longer to get back to a comparable place on the ladder, and your income will be significantly less for a time, but I think it is worth it to make the switch. You will be happier and more able to be a gift to others, including your coworkers and your family.

When you get that first entry level position in a graphic design firm, you will work harder and strive to produce a better product, not because you have to, but because you want to. Doing what you love gives you a feeling of satisfaction. This is a gift that you give to yourself. It is important to want to achieve personal satisfaction. That, in my mind, is a measure of success.

If you are a happier person in your job, you are bound to be happier person outside the job. You will be a happier person around your children—better able to support them in their activities.

My personal success took a long time to achieve, but I feel very happy now for having stuck it out for the long haul. I am a managing partner of my medical center and happy as a clam. Other doctors come to me and ask how I did it. I just smile at them because I know something they do not.

"Success requires patience and hard work."

"Success is about perseverance and patience."

"Success is a by-product of hard honest work."

As much as I greatly desired to be able to play the piano, I never could master it. I didn't have what it takes. When I was in high school, my classmates and I dressed, walked, and combed our hair like James Dean. We would hold parties and dance to rock 'n' roll. If you played in a band, then you became a kind of semihero yourself. So I tried and tried, but never could play more than a few chords on the piano. It was one thing I was never going to be good at. But by chance, I discovered that I could understand chemicals and bioscience. They came to me as easily as some people can sit down at the piano for the first time and play it. At least I can definitely enjoy singing with the church choir, men assembly, or with Men Tet's group. So becoming a doctor was natural for me. I was good at it. Find something—anything that you can master or excel in and enjoy—and this should be your life work. Too many children follow career paths that have nothing to do with what the child will joyfully thrive doing. Too many young people follow a bleak, sterile, and joyless path toward money, security, and wealth. I have no disagreement with working for a living. But I have much against working and hating your work. So take some thought about what you do well and enjoy. Decide on what is fun. And if you pursue that, you will be following a better path. Because if you enjoy your work, chances are that you will be outstanding at it and achieve a level of excellence so far above someone who hates his job no matter how much money he makes at doing it. Doing work that you love each day offers a gift in return to the one who gave you the original talent, ability, skill, savvy, and knack to get it right. Using the gifts that were given to you to their fullest makes you a wonderful and most highly appreciated gift to him.

CHAPTER NINE

Work

When I pondered the value of work, I remembered some experiences from my church. Most churches support missionaries who go to third world countries to help children, old people, everyone, really. But what do they do for these people?

Every year, teenagers and young adults come to church on Sunday mornings to tell us that they are planning a mission to Zimbabwe or Nicaragua. They then ask for money to pay for their traveling expenses. To avoid appearing stingy or unsupportive of mission work, most churchgoers contribute some money.

Unless you ask one of these young people directly about their day-to-day activities on the mission, you may be blindly giving money to someone's potential vacation. For all we know, they are getting up at eleven in the morning and partying late into the night, only occasionally building a tent or distributing foodstuff.

Now I'm not saying that missionaries are slackers. They do good work, all of them. Charity is a very important endeavor. I'm also not saying that it is wasteful to contribute money to a missionary trip. The point I am trying to make here is that money is not something to be given for nothing. If one of these kids wants to mow my lawn or wash my car, I will gladly donate funds to their mission trip. It is important to learn the value of money.

A dedicated, missionary-minded young lady from our church contacted us recently. She wished to raise funds to buy a birthday present for her husband. She offered to do some housework for us to earn the money.

One of their core values is the worth and importance of raising fund by working to earn them. By using their talents and gifts, they have been able to help other less fortunate families both in this country and overseas. The sacrifice of their time, energies, and funds has enabled them to give to others less fortunate than themselves. In this manner, they themselves have received the gift of doing labor for a good cause, receiving the gift of funds in order to be able to serve, as well as give of their financial largesse to those in need.

With this model for raising funds for ministry, all parties benefit and receive gifts. The party whose house is cleaned regularly receives the gift of a clean, antiseptic home. The parties doing the labor receive the gifts of good, honest work; the appreciation of those served; income well-earned; and sufficient funds to share with others. The parties receiving the financial gifts benefit by those things that money can buy, so all parties benefit all the way up and down the line.

Three students who attend a Christian high school wanted to raise money to travel to the Dominican Republic to do mission work. So their motivation was for the greater good, outside of themselves, for others less fortunate, a most commendable enterprise. They were journeying there to give the gift of their time and faith to do mission work for the school. My son was among those three students. I was so very proud of the young man that he had become.

The students offered to clean the homes of some of our church members in order to raise the funds that they needed. The ladies at our church who availed themselves of the students' services were very pleased and satisfied with the work the students did. The women were doubly pleased because by having their yards cleaned, they were also contributing to God's work. By employing the young people who were mission bound, these women were also doing God's work.

In this instance, there was gifting on all sides. The students were gifted with the opportunity to serve both at home doing the cleaning, plus abroad doing mission work, plus they received the funds that they earned with their labors. The women who hired the students were gifted with clean yards and the satisfaction of furthering God's work. They also had the double satisfaction of paying monies to deserving students who were hardworking and the delayed satisfaction of having their monies used to benefit others who were less fortunate than themselves. Moreover, they did not have to journey outside their own homes nor do anything more than pay monies for honest labors to be able to reap this satisfaction.

The Dominicans received both the presence and labors of the students. Those less fortunate in the Dominican Republic received the gifts of the students because others had gifted the students. By working for church members and raising funds, the students were able to go to the Caribbean—to a nation less fortunate than our own. They received multiple gifts: self-knowledge; the chance to personally help others less fortunate; the experience of being on their own likely for the first time in their lives; and the opportunity to embody the lessons the church had taught them to live their faith in a real, palpable way.

The students were a gift to all they touched: the church ladies whose homes they cleaned, the parents of the students who were so proud of their children, the Dominican families who received their labors and efforts and love, and their church since their efforts reflected well upon their school. The students also grew greatly in life experiences, self-confidence, faith in both God and themselves, and in empathy for others. This shared experience brought the students joy, satisfaction, and mutual well-being and pride in church, family, and self. It also gave each of them a real connection to all mankind—both those in a more exalted position and those in less privileged circumstances.

Life is a gift. What we choose to do with it, and how we live our lives is our gift to others and God. Let us always be aware of that and strive to live our lives in a godly manner. Let us be a gift to those around us every day—those we love and those we do not know yet as friends—for we are all God's creatures and equal under our God.

While my children were growing up, they worked for their allowance by doing chores around the home. As they got older, we were able to give them other tasks such as errands and chauffeuring younger siblings. My wife and I felt that they needed to understand that money is not a free commodity. We instead wanted them to understand the value of both work and finances. I believe that my children learned the value of an hour's worth of work. So even when young missionaries are planning to travel for good, charitable reasons, they still need to understand that the way to provide their support is to work for it.

Ethical practices in business are very important, too. The doctor I started out working for, Doctor Mentor, was not the most ethical employer. He was a very good doctor, but he had a high turnover rate. He would string me along, telling me that he wanted to make me a partner in his business. He told me this for years because he believed that it was what I wanted to hear.

This doctor dangled a carrot in front of me to maintain my interest in his medical center. Being a partner would have been great, but I did not need to be a partner. The point is that he was making empty promises. Doctor Mentor never intended to make me a partner in his business. In the end, this relationship was lose-lose. It was a loss for me because I did not achieve the promised partnership, and it was a loss for Doctor Mentor because I left his medical center. I moved on to other avenues in my career and ultimately established a rival medical center.

There was a well-educated, hardworking physician's assistant at Doctor Mentor's medical center who was also rather disenchanted by Doctor Mentor's ethics. One day, I got a call from him. He asked me out to lunch.

We met in a little café, and he told me about how unhappy he was at Doctor Mentor's medical center. "Could I come to work for you?" he asked.

"Absolutely!" I said. So he came to work for me, which was a great deal for me because he is very good at his job. That was in 1989, and he is still with my center. The patients love him, and I pay him well. This is a definite win-win. He is such a gift to me that, when we bought back our medical center, I made him a partner in the business. This was a gift to him, and it has the added bonus of giving him a personal stake in our medical center.

I think making employees partners is a good practice for this exact reason. When they have personal stakes in the business, they are more likely to work harder. This is a gift to the medical center. Partnerships are gifts to the partners.

An ethical and healthy attitude to take when approaching one's job is to view it as more than just a job. If you are happy at your place of work, you are more likely to play an active and productive role. I care for my employees and like to see that they are happy. As far as I can tell, they all view their jobs as careers. I think the gift of partnerships assists in that. It makes me happy to see that they enjoy what they do.

When an employee seems to be unhappy, we address the matter head on. It is important to do what you love because that is what will make you happy. It is not always an option to have the job you want, but you can try and aim for it. Take classes, gain experience, and do what it takes to obtain the job that will lead to a fulfilling career for you. In the end, this will make for a better life. It seems to me that a person who is happy at work goes home happy. That man or woman is a better husband or wife and a more approachable father or mother. Having a healthy balance between career and home life is important.

Another aspect relating to work is the fact that we are facing failure sometime. Failure can be a discouraging event. However, failure can turn into positive thinking. One may learn from his or her mistake and getting better later on. Failure is an event—not a destiny—for God has a better plan.

We knew that our house needed new roofing and repairs to both the trim and the deck railings. My sister Sylvia and her husband Pete are familiar with construction since they have renovated properties in Maine. In the process of renovation, they employed gifted craftsman. We invited Sylvia and Pete to visit us.

While they were here, we sought their advice regarding repairs to our home. They recommended a carpenter, Sam, who had been helping Pete do renovations in Maine. Sam had worked with Pete in the past and would likely do so in the future. Based on their referral, he agreed to do the repairs on our home.

When Sam arrived, he brought another carpenter to be his helper. While they were making the repairs, the two of them lived in the basement of our house. We treated them like members of our family. They worked long hours—from just after sunrise to almost sunset. They worked almost every day of the week—Monday through Saturdays.

In the beginning, they were hard working and conscientious, putting their hearts and souls into their work. Even so, due to some unanticipated tasks, it took them almost six months to complete all that needed to be done. Sam and his helper both became friends over the course of our business relationship. He gifted us with his dedication to quality and detail, as well as his hard work. Highly detail oriented, he promised to make certain all work was done just right, and he constantly pondered how to do the best possible job.

We gifted Sam with our trust, our open hearts and the peace and warmth of our home. We gave him and his helper the gift of honest work to complete an abode, and we also shared home-cooked meals with both of them almost every day. It was a mutually enriching, symbiotic relationship for us all.

Unfortunately, reviewing the original construction of our home with the gift of hindsight, we realized that it was built neither soundly nor adequately. This occurred because numerous construction workers had been neither sufficiently dedicated nor honest nor committed to quality in order to fully and adequately performs their tasks. The construction crew that initially built our home was neither a gift to us, nor any other homeowner whose home they erected.

We need good, honest, hardworking, skilled, and committed workers, not only in the construction trades, but in other businesses as well. Providing quality work or well-built products for fair compensation is a gift to all parties involved—both worker and consumer. One is gifted with a living wage, while the other receives worth and value for his or her expenditures.

This vignette illustrates how my sister Sylvia and her husband Pete are a gift to us. By sharing with us their wisdom, advice, and recommendations for good worker, they gifted us indeed. We are allowed to see these gifts around us every day as a result.

Unfortunately, over time, Sam and his helper became less effective and less productive, extending their hours inappropriately. This is another example of a relationship that soured over time. They were no longer as great a gift to us.

They started well but did not finish well. Unfortunately, we see that a lot in workplaces. People make good promises but many times unable to complete the work satisfactorily.

"Start well and finish well."

To be a gift to each other, we need to follow that.

It is important to work hard and work smart. This means prioritizing your time both at work and at home. If you manage your time at work properly, you can do your tasks more quickly. This may mean that you can spend more time at home.

With more time at home, you can be with your children more. Your children will appreciate the time and energy you put into family life.

When my first child started kindergarten, I decided that I needed to better divide my time between home and work. From that first day, I started working half days and continued to do so until my youngest child finished the twelfth grade. Not all people can do this, but it is not about the amount of time you spend with your children. It is about the quality of that time. I made the effort to be there for all my children's extracurricular activities. I attended all recitals and athletic games. My children appreciated this. I think it has had a significant impact on the relationship I have with each of my children. Even if you cannot take half days off from work, make time for your family after work and on weekends. Be sure to take family vacations.

Using your time wisely at work enables you to be more productive in less time. This applies to other tasks as well. If you plan out your tasks and establish a list of priorities, you can accomplish more in a day than you might have expected. This will leave time for other activities and important errands. The free time can be spent on exercise, grocery trips, and the all-important time with your children. That is what I call working smart.

Working hard is also important. Focus plays a major role in this. Studious effort to develop your talents can lead to a happy work life. When we work hard and do good work, we become a shining light to other people. You become a blessing to other people, and others receive the benefit of your hard and good work.

Every person has certain unique talents, some with a few talents, and others with several talents. It is not important how many talents you have, but what you do with those talents. You should not be lazy, but instead develop and maximize the talents that you have. Ecclesiastes clearly advises us that work is a gift from God, and we get satisfaction and joy out of the fruit of our labor.

Your work ethic determines your work life. How you work will affect how you spend your personal life. So you see, it is important to work hard and work smart. Dr. Martin Luther King, Jr., once said, "All labor that uplifts humanity has dignity and importance and should be undertaken with painstaking excellence." If you are happy and fulfilled in your career, you will be more amiable and friendly at home.

"Do what you love and love what you do; that is the key to a happy work life."

"Working hard is a virtue."

Using our gifts and working hard is an act of obedience to our Creator. God has given each person the gift of work. According to Ecclesiastes, we clearly find satisfaction in labors during our life on earth. We need to be happy and enjoy our labors. Labor will result in a blessing of both wealth and possessions. This, too, we should enjoy. It is pleasing to our Lord when we work our best. Furthermore, Matthew 5:16 tells us, "In the same way, let your light shine before men, that they may see your good deeds and praise your Father in heaven."

However, we should not be slavish, working day and night, simply to accumulate wealth and possessions. Instead, we should work smart and manage our time more conscientiously and effectively. If you work slavishly, you lose focus, sleep, satisfaction, and your health.

When I had young children, I made a conscious decision to alter my work schedule in order to be available to them. I compressed more work into a shorter day to be able to leave work earlier. In this manner, I was able to participate in or attend my children's extracurricular activities. Whether I attended my daughter's soccer games or my son's basketball games, coached my second son's baseball team, or attended my youngest daughter's music recitals, each and every one of those occasions was a blessing and a gift to me. In return, it was a blessing and a gift to each of my children to experience my love and support through my presence. So in each instance, it was a gift for us both. Since I changed my work schedule, I have enjoyed my work more and because I believe I am gifting all whom I touch with my skills, concern, and good intentions.

A positive wrinkle in your professional career can be modifying or varying the type of work at which you excel. If you are a systems designer, consider taking on other roles so you can not only empathize with your colleagues but also broaden your skills and experience and keep your chosen field of work fresh and interesting.

Everyone is particularly good at something. But breaking out of your routine can give you a new perspective so that your work continues to be a gift both to you and to those with whom you work.

I've always enjoyed my encounters with patients, whether for minor ailments, major illnesses, or simply health maintenance.

However, after working as a family physician for many years, I find the day-to-day tasks of the job can become boring due to all the routine and the repetitiveness of the tasks involved. Boredom can lead to burnout depression and loss of interest in a job.

Listen to story of a patient of mine, who wrote a letter to me. She said, "I am not very sure of the time when I became your patient. I do know that I was on my knees in prayer, and the Lord showed me this office. I thank God for you. I know that there is a significant reason for my being placed under your care and that he has a divine purpose." Indeed, God is in control.

Since my undergraduate years, I have been interested in conducting research studies. At that time, I worked with a famous anthropologist. Both he and I received the gift of working together. I was exposed to the intricacies of conducting research, and he received my labors on his behalf. As his protégé, I received the gift of his extensive experience.

I learned his methodologies and received his guidance on conducting research studies step by step. In addition, he gave me daily feedback on effectively completing the detailed steps necessary to adhere to the stringent requirements of the research. He was gifted by my focused exuberance and dedication, my willingness to learn and function as a skilled set of hands implementing his directives. In me, he had a willing, though junior, partner in his scientific research and his efforts to push the scientific envelope. As a consequence of this experience, my vision expanded to encompass the desire to start doing clinical research in my area of medical expertise. This is one way of avoiding burnout.

However, breaking into clinical trials and medical research is quite difficult. It is most difficult to break into the rarefied air of conducting clinical studies for the federal government under the auspices of the National Institutes of Health (NIH) or their federal contractors. To get involved in clinical research as a principal investigator, I needed a grant and a contract from NIH or perhaps a pharmaceutical company. Not a single company would give me a grant due to my lack of experience.

I found myself in a catch-22 situation, between a rock and a hard place. I couldn't do research without a grant and a contract, and I didn't merit a contract without experience doing research. People from several pharmaceutical companies tried to assist me in landing a grant but to no avail. At the time, it seemed as if I would never be able to break into research.

As a God-fearing man, I believe that God has a plan for each person. I also believe that God's timing is perfect, even though we may not be able to see it at the time. So I was patient, comfortable in God's grace. However, maintaining that patience required effort.

One day, I received a communiqué from the University of Texas in Houston. The communication asked if I would be interested in participating in a clinical trial researching high blood pressure. This communication came out of the blue. The large blood pressure trial Texas researchers were conducting was sponsored by NIH and needed more investigators. Without any hesitation whatsoever, I signed up to participate. That initial study got me in the door.

Ever since that day, I have been in the database of those on a short list for potential investigators to participate in upcoming clinical trials. This involvement in clinical research has helped me tremendously in avoiding potential burnout from my work as a family physician. The new research with which I have been involved has also given me cutting-edge knowledge of medical advances that have trickled down into my daily practice. Moreover, the variety has made my regular work more enjoyable.

Our performance in the NIH study was very satisfactory due, in large part, to our ability to enroll and complete the trial with a significant number of patients. Our positive track record has greatly facilitated the opportunity to get additional grants and contracts over the years. As a consequence of these ongoing successes, our clinical studies research office has grown, adding both skilled employees and office space, while providing additional jobs to the local community.

Our past successes enable us to expand our inventory of ongoing studies, add clinical personnel as needed, provide services to our test subjects, contribute to new findings based on our clinical test results, serve as principal investigators for pharmaceutical companies, and help our local communities as a medical resource center. Our clinical research site has been and remains today a gift to multiple sponsors, pharmaceutical companies, patients, and the research community.

I was driving to work looking forward to a routine workload under a glared sun. As I neared the Woodrow Wilson Bridge coming from Virginia, I noticed that the inside fast lane that I was driving in was under construction. One could still drive in the lane, but the concrete construction barriers along the left side of the road only left the bare minimum of space to drive through. I slowed down as a cautionary measure. Unfortunately, one of the concrete sections was out of line, it was sticking out into my lane. I moved to my right as soon as I saw it, but the Toyota Camry Sedan I was driving clipped the edge of the barrier, forcing me to ricochet sharply to the right. Unseen by me, a large eighteen-wheeler was passing me on the right just as I hit the barrier on my left. I found myself in a horrendous and frightening situation. The Camry slammed against the eighteen-wheeler with great force and then jammed back against the unyielding concrete. Again and again, my car took ugly hits from these objects, banging back and forth. The sound of screeching metal on metal and the barriers was deafening. I truly expected this was to be my end and closed my eyes in surrender. Sudden and complete silence followed. I opened my eyes. Looking around, there were no cars behind me or beside me. I was safe, although in a car that might be considered completely totaled—judging by huge gouged, ripped, and smashed metal along on both sides of the Camry. I pulled over to the open unattended shoulder, shaking with the understandable adrenaline. The driver of the eighteen-wheeler circled back and stopped. He claimed that I was alive because he had just installed a set of metal truck side bumpers designed to deflect cars from hitting the side of his vehicle. I thanked him for stopping. But more than that, I thanked the Lord for letting me stay alive on this earth for a bit longer. I was grateful for what I felt was his ultimate blessing; I was thankful for my life. For no matter what gifts one has been given or not given, if one has the gift of life, anything is possible. Without the blessing of life, it stands to reason that nothing is possible.

CHAPTER TEN
Blessing

Throughout the course of your life, you receive many blessings and hopefully give many blessings to others. When you get right down to it, every day on this earth is a blessing from God, regardless of your religion. We must approach life with this attitude in mind, and that is really what this book's message. Be a blessing to others, and you will be blessed in return. We need each other. That is the essential truth of life. I count every member of my family as a blessing, as well as each friend, each turn of good fortune.

We are all blessed with life from our Creator, and we live our best, and he orchestrates our daily life. As we get older, we see that God has blessed us in all things. Today, you let someone pass you in traffic. Tomorrow, someone holds a door for you when your hands are full. I believe that if you do good things in life, good things will happen to you or good opportunities will appear.

I was blessed by having a caring, loving, and godly mother who imparted her wisdom to me. Some may not have that privilege, but God can provide the blessing of wisdom through any source. The question is whether we will listen and accept that advice and follow through.

For example, look at my friend, the physician assistant. We were friends while working for Doctor Mentor. We helped each other then. Later, he came to work with me. He is great at his job, and I appreciate him every day. We are gifts to each other.

Having supportive siblings who are behind you, whether you succeed or fail, is a blessing. My sisters and brothers were gifts in many ways to me. You may not have brothers and sisters, but you can receive support from friends, neighbors, and members of the church.

Your children may be another source of support. If you guide them well and help them, they will later take care of you when you are elderly. They could just shove you off into a sad nursing home before you need it, or they could take you into their own home and treat you with the respect you showed them in earlier years.

We were blessed with four wonderful children. My wife and I have had a blessed time raising our children and training them, giving them a strong foundation based on Christian standards so that as adults they will not stray from the truth.

The blessing of our oldest daughter is that she has a sense of leadership, a keen discernment, and strong convictions. She is married to a godly man, a family man who lives and sets an example of what a head of household should be. We were even blessed with two grandsons and two granddaughters, who are being raised according to the biblical standard.

We are also blessed by my older daughter's husband. He is a studious and conscientious young man, and I can see why my daughter chose him. His entry in our lives changed the nature of my relationship to my daughter, of course, and our relationship has shown me things about the nature of parenting and being a father I had not seen before. I have two sons, and my son-in-law has related to me in a way that is different than my sons; he has shown me things about myself that I never knew. He is a gift to me, to my family, and of course, to my daughter and grandchildren.

We are also blessed with our older son who has studied hard and is using his talents well and appropriately. He has served as a technology guru, as my wife called it, to our family members by creating a family blog. It is a joy to see how he exercises obedience to God and to his parents and shows his love to his siblings and his parents and his loyalty and care to his friends.

How about the blessing of having a younger daughter who is beautiful outside and very sweet inside? Her desire to help others by going on mission trips and sharing her musical talent to comfort the needy is beautiful to see. She will be able to combine the ministry of medicine and music, serving many people, which is pleasing to our Creator.

The blessing continues with our fourth child, the younger son. He is such a likable person who loves and cares for so many people and has been a blessing to many of his friends. His positive attitude and his love and respect for his parents are indeed a gift.

I had the blessing of marrying a lovely wife who fears God and is always obedient to his guidance. She has been always by my side, and she has helped to make me a better person. She loves our children dearly and never fails to call and to encourage each one of them.

You get what you give. The songs all talk about this principle because it is a universal truth. We find this truth in the treasured texts of every generation. Treat others the way in which you want to be treated. This truth remains over the course of time like an enduring pennant holding its own through snowstorms and wind.

We only get one chance at life, so why not make your life fun and meaningful?

"Every day is a gift from our Creator."

We do him a disservice when we treat each day as another round of misery. Naturally, we all hit our ruts and bouts of unhappiness, but this can be overcome. Do what makes you happy and help others; you will then become a gift to God as well as to the others around you.

My wife tells me that I am the most positive person she knows. This is because I am happy in everything I do. When you approach life with a positive attitude, hardships do not seem so difficult. We can push through anything. I know that my family will be with me in everything I do.

With them, I feel like Superman. That must sound trite, but it is true.

My goal in this book is to help others see that every moment in our lifetime is a gift, even those awful moments we wish to forget. Those sore spots carry with them lessons. After all, we learn by making mistakes. That's the simple truth.

Our parents try to keep us from harm. They try to teach us right from wrong, but in the end, we learn by experience. As much as I might want to teach you about the gifts of life and how to be a gift to others, you will really only learn this by being your own person and making your own mistakes.

You may have a fight with your wife or perhaps say something you should not have said. At some point, you will realize the mistake you have made. When you make up, you may find that the argument was a blessing in disguise since making up after it drew you closer together. That is the nature of life. As they say, God works in mysterious ways.

The blessing of having a relationship with our Creator, our God, is the ultimate blessing. The fact that human beings can even have that relationship with their Creator is a blessing by itself. When one's life is intertwined, then the social, the intellectual, and the spiritual aspects of your life are fully integrated; you will be able to live a whole, balanced, and successful life. You can then appreciate your limitations and yet able to do your best with what has been given to you. Your goal is no longer to please yourself but to please your neighbors and your God.

Innate in each individual is the capacity for both good and evil, for making right and wrong decisions. As long as you try to seek the good, to make the right decisions, you will be fine. You might even figure out how best to be a gift to others and, in doing so, become a gift to your Creator. In the very act of trying, we succeed.

CONCLUSION

In the final analysis, I must conclude here by stating that I deeply believe that my total worth on this earth comes from how well I helped others. I believe that you are what you give—that you are known by what you give others. I feel that my true measure is the extent to which I gave the gift of myself—my time, support, and love to others in this world.

If it is true that you get what you give, then how much you give is how much you are. The ten-year-old son of a good friend once asked me, "How do you find love in this world?" My reply was simple, "You only have to give love, and it will find you."

And so my conclusion is equally simple: make your life a gift to others and a multitude of gifts will return to you. Albert Einstein was once quoted as saying something akin to "God does not play dice with the universe." I believe this pertains to the basis of his theories about action and equal reaction. I believe that Albert Einstein meant that God has created an ordered system of balances and love—that if you give gifts, you will eventually receive gifts.

This is quite simple, really, but sometimes the simplest things are the ones we forget easiest and soonest. So I write this reminder. May this book be a reason for you to stop and think how you can be a gift to others. And by no means does this refer only to material gifts— although by itself, material gifts have positive impact on people.

Specifically, we seek to be a gift to each other in our relationship at home, in the workplace, or even in our social setting. I am not saying that you should be a pushover about everything; allow yourself to be taken advantage of. No, I am just saying that kindness is not weakness. Try to keep yourself open to all opportunities in life wherein you can add value to a friend, a wife, a son or daughter, a stranger. Because in the end, the value you give will ultimately be the value of your own life. So strive and endeavor in all things to offer pure value without thought of profit or return—to always be a gift to others.

www.ingramcontent.com/pod-product-compliance
Lightning Source LLC
Chambersburg PA
CBHW051546120626
46551CB00013B/1387